T0149580

THE GIFT OF LIFE COMMUNITY HOME INC PRESENTS:

TEEN PREGNANCY BEFORE, DURING, AND AFTER!

HOLISTIC CHOICES TO MAKE BEFORE THE OUTCOME, REAL TALK!

THIS BOOK IS INTENDED TO DISCUSS THE ISSUES OF TEEN PREGNANCY TO TEENAGERS BEFORE IT HAPPENS, IF IT HAPPENS, AND WHAT TO DO AFTER IT HAPPENS, FROM A HOLISTIC VIEW

TEEN PREGNANCY BEFORE, DURING, AND AFTER!

HOLISTIC CHOICES TO MAKE BEFORE THE OUTCOME, REAL TALK!

YOLANDA V. HENDERSON N.D., C.H.C

TEEN PREGNANCY BEFORE, DURING, AND AFTER!
HOLISTIC CHOICES TO MAKE BEFORE THE OUTCOME, REAL TALK!

iUniverse books may be ordered through booksellers or by contacting:

iUniverse
1663 Liberty Drive
Bloomington, IN 47403
www.iuniverse.com
1-800-Authors (1-800-288-4677)

Because of the dynamic nature of the Internet, any web addresses or links contained in this book may have changed since publication and may no longer be valid. The views expressed in this work are solely those of the author and do not necessarily reflect the views of the publisher, and the publisher hereby disclaims any responsibility for them.

Any people depicted in stock imagery provided by Thinkstock are models, and such images are being used for illustrative purposes only.
Certain stock imagery © Thinkstock.

ISBN: 978-1-5320-1206-8 (sc)
ISBN: 978-1-5320-1207-5 (hc)
ISBN: 978-1-5320-1208-2 (e)

Print information available on the last page.

iUniverse rev. date: 11/23/2016

Contents

Acknowledgment

TO MY HANDSOME HUSBAND NORMAL HENDERSON jr., DEAREST GRANDMOTHER, AND CHILDREN: PATIENCE, NINA, GERALD, JAYLEN, KING, AND NORMAL III. TO OTHERS FOR ALLOWING ME TO MAKE YOUTH MISTAKES, MOTHER AND FATHER, SISTERS AND BROTHERS, HOST OF AUNTS, UNCLES, COUSINS, A HOST OF FAMILY OF MY AWESOME HUSBAND, AND FRIENDS!

Foreword

THIS BOOK IS DEDICATED TO TEENAGERS AND PARENTS OF ALL ETHNIC GROUPS, RELIOUS BACKGROUNDS, RACE, SOCIAL CLASS, OR SEX. SOME PREGNANCIES ARE NOT ALL PLANNED. SOME ARE FORCED, AND SOME PREGNANCIES ARE SLIP UPS OF SOCIAL CLASS. A VARIETY OF THE FACTORS ARE THE SAME. MOST TEENS THAT HAVE SEX ARE IN THE PROCESS OF BECOMING TEEN PARENTS. MOST DROP OUT OF SCHOOL, RUN AWAY FROM HOME, AND SOME START TO USE ILLEGAL DRUGS. OUR GOAL IS THAT THIS BOOK, OUR FACILITY, OUR STAFF, AND YOU WILL BE ABLE TO HELP TEENS START OVER BRAND NEW. THIS BOOK CONTAINS INFORMATION ABOUT HOLISTIC (the complete life balance including Joy/confidence, social life, relationships, finances, education, career, health, physical activity, home cooking, home environment, creativity, and spirituality) TEEN PARENTING, PREGANCY EDUCATION, LIFE SKILLS, FAMILY VIOLENCE, TEEN RELATIONSHIPS, STDS, SEX, AND SPIRIUTALLITY. IF YOU FIND YOURSELF READING THIS FORWARD AND KNOW OF A TEENAGER BOY OR GIRL, GIVE THIS AS A GIFT, IT JUST MIGHT CHANGE A LIFE AND YOU COULD BE THE REASON.

HOLISTICICALLY WE RELY ON PRIMARY AND SECONDARY FOODS TO DRIVE US AS HUMANS. PRIMARY FOOD GOES BEYOND THE PLATE, NURTURING US ON A DEEPER LEVEL.

The four main primary foods are relationships, Education/career (depending on your age), physical activity, and spirituality.

SECONDARY FOODS ARE WHAT WE ACTULLY PUT INTO OUR BODIES FOR NUTRITION.

IF OUR PRIMARY FOODS ARE NOT IN ORDER IT CAN CAUSE OUR SECONDARY FOODS TO BE POOR. HINTS THE CRAVINGS OF FOODS THAT ARE NOT GOOD FOR US LEADING TO ALL SORTS OF HEALTH ISSUES, AND UNWANTED BUT CONTROLABLE LIFESTYLE CHOICES.

Before

You decide pregnancy is an
option read this book!

PART 1

AM I PREGNANT?
RISKY BEHAVIORS

15 MINUTES OF PLEASURE,
NINE MONTHS OF PAIN,
A BOY OR A GIRL TO NAME,
HE/SHE DON'T EVEN KNOW MY NAME,
THIS ALL STARTED FROM A CHILDISH GAME.
HE/SHE SAID HE/SHE LOVED ME,
HE/SHE CAN'T HANDLE HIS/HER RESPONSIBILITY.
DREAMS OF SUCCESS, COLLEGE AND FAME,
NOW ALL I HEAR IS THE BABY BOY OR GIRL SCREAMS.
IF I COULD TAKE BACK THE HANDS OF TIME,
I WOULD KEEP THE FREEDOM THAT
WAS RIGHTFULLY MINE.
-YOLANDA THIBODEAUX

AM I PREGNANT?

COCO's DIARY ENTRY:

MARCH 17, 2000

DEAR DIARY,

I DIDN'T LISTEN WHEN MY MOTHER WARNED ME ABOUT SEX. I TOLD HER SHE HAD NOTHING TO WORRY ABOUT. THAT WASN'T MY FOCUS. NOW IM SUFFERING FROM WHAT I BELIEVE IS MORNING SICKNESS. I CAN BARELY GET THROUGH FIRST PERIOD WITHOUT RUNNING TO THE BATHROOM. A COUPLE OF WEEKS AGO WHEN I WROTE I EXPERIEMENTED WITH SEX, MAYBE THAT WAS THE WRONG THING TO DO. BUT RUSSEL TOLD ME IF I LOVED HIM I WOULD PROVE IT. NOW IM CRAVING ALL KINDS OF WEIRD FOODS. I'VE SEEN THE EPISODES ON MAURY AND THE SHOWS ABOUT GUYS THAT JUST TELL GIRLS THINGS TO GET THEM TO HAVE SEX. HOW COULD I HAVE BEEN SO STUPID?

IF YOU ARE HAVING SEX AND NOT ON BIRTH CONTROL OR USING CONDOMS YOU ARE AT RISK OFBECOMING PREGNAT. MANY YOUNG GIRLS AND GUYS ARE TOLD OF THE OUTCOMES OF HAVING SEX. SOME OF THE SIGNS OF PREGNANCY ARE MORNING SICKNESS, FREQUENT URINATION, FOOD CRAVINGS, AMENORREAH (ABSENCE OF MENUSTRATION) TINGLING, TENDER SWOLLEN BREAST AND OTHERS LATER DISCUSSED IN PART 3 OF THIS BOOK. THE ONLY REAL WAYS TO KNOW IF YOU OR YOUR GIRLFRIEND IS PREGNANT IS TO TAKE A PREGANCY TEST, (PROPERLY), OR TAKE A BLOOD TEST GIVEN BY A DOCTOR.

RISKY BEHAVIORS

COCO'S DIARY ENTRY:

MARCH 20, 2000

DEAR DIARY,

I CAN'T TAKE IT ANYMORE. I HAVE TO GET A TEST. MY MOM WOULD KILL ME IF I TOLD HER THAT I NEEDED TO TAKE A PREGNANCY TEST. SHE TOLD ME IF I EVER THOUGHT ABOUT SEX LET HER KNOW THEN SHE WOULD TAKE ME TO GET ON BIRTH CONTROL. NO ONE WOULD BELIEVE WE USED A CONDOM AND IT BROKE. I CAN TAKE THE MONEY I SAVED, AND BUY ME A TEST. I COULD TAKE THE TEST AT SCHOOL OR AT RUSSELS HOUSE. RUSSEL WANTS ME TO COME OVER HIS HOUSE TONIGHT WHILE HIS PARENTS ARE AWAY. MAYBE I SHOULD TELL MY MOM IM SLEEPING OVER AT CRYSTAL'S APARTMENT (SINCE SHE MOVED OUT WITH HER BOYFRIEND). SHE CAN PRETEND THAT SHE IS HER MOTHER AND EVERYTHING WOULD BE GREAT. WOW, THIS IS RISKY BUT IT MAYBE SOME TIME TO SHOW RUSSEL THAT HE DOESN'T HAVE TO LOOK AT ANOTHER GIRL AGAIN...☺

SOME RISKY BEHAVIORS OF TEEN SEX PREGNANCY INCLUDES:

- LIEING TO PARENTS,
- TRYING TO MAKE SOMEONE LIKE YOU,
- USING ILLEGAL DRUGS,
- DRINKING ALCHOL,
- SKIPPING SCHOOL TO BE WITH YOUR BOYFRIEND/ GIRLFRIEND.
- NOT USING CONDOMS, OR PROSTITUTION.
  THESE RISKS DOES NOT ONLY LEAD TO TEEN PREGNANCY, BUT OTHER RISK INCLUDES STI'S (SEXUAL TRANSMITTED

INFECTIONS) SUCH AS GONNOREAH, CLAMIDIAH. IN ADDITION, MORE SERIOUS STDS (SEXUALLY TRANSMITTED DIESEASE), LIKE HIV, AIDS, AND HERPES. THESE DIESESES NEVER GO AWAY.

TAKE A MOMENT TO THINK ABOUT THESE RISKS ABOVE. WRITE ANOTHER RISK THAT YOU MAYIS FEEL IMPORTANT.

1. AN IMPORTANT RISK IS… _____

    _____

2. THIS IS RISKY BECAUSE…._____

    _____

3. IS _____ REALLY WORTH ANY OF THESE RISKS?

4. SPIRITUALITY: USE A PRAYER JOURNAL OR WRITE BELOW TO THE GOD OF YOUR FAMILY'S BELIEF TO ASK FOR HELP IN SUSTAINING FROM PRMARTIAL SEX. WE ARE REMINDED IN SCRIPTURE.

PSALMS 28:7 THE LORD IS MY STRENTH AND MY SHIELD; MY HEART TRUST IN HIM, AND I AM HELPED.

_____

_____

_____

_____

_____

_____

_____

_____

_____

_____

_____

_____

_____

CHAPTER 1

WHY DO I WANT A CHILD?

I CANNOT COUNT THE GOOD PEOPLE I KNOW
WHO TO MY MIND WOULD BE EVEN BETTER
IF THEY SPENT THEIR SPIRITS TO THE STUDY
OF THEIR OWN HUNGERS

-M.F.K. FISHER

FACTORS AT THE ROOT OF TEEN PREGNANCY

DEVELOP INTEREST IN LIFE AS YOU SEE IT;
IN PEOPLE, THINGS, LITERATURE, MUSIC-
THE WORLD IS SO RICH, SIMPLY THROBBING
WITH RICH TREASURES, BEAUTIFUL SOULS
AND INTERESTING PEOPLE. FORGET
YOURSELF.

-HENRY MILLER

COCO'S DIARY ENTRY:

MARCH 21, 2000

DEAR DIARY,

LAST NIGHT I WENT TO RUSSELS' HOUSE. I TOLD HIM THAT I MIGHT BE PREGNANT. HE WAS REALLY UPSET WITH ME. HE TOLD ME IT MAY NOT BE HIS. I KNOW THAT IF I WAS IT WERE HIS. HE FINALLY AGREEDTHAT I SHOULD TAKE A PREGNANCY TEST. HE TOLD ME THAT HAVING A KID WOULD MESS UP HIS CHANCE TO GO TO COLLEGE NEXT YEAR HE HAD GOTTEN A FULL FOOTBALL SCHOLARSHIP TO UCLA. I THOUGHT ABOUT HOW IT COULD AFFECT MY LIFE, I WAS ONLY A SOPHMORE IN HIGH SCHOOL. I COULD NOT EVEN WORK UNTIL MY NEXT BIRTHDAY IN JANUARY. THE THOUGHT OF TAKING CARE OF A BABY I COULD NOT POSSIBLY TAKE CARE OF WAS REALLY SCARY, ON THE OTHER HAND, I AM KINDA EXCITED ABOUT WHAT THE CHILD WOULD LOOK LIKE. MYBEAUTIFUL BROWN EYES, HIS CUTE BUTTON NOSE. WHY AM I THINKING OF THIS RIGHT NOW? I am ALREADY ON THE VARSITY CHEERLEADING SQUAD, MATH TEAM, AND TAKING PRE-COLLEGE COURSES. I HAVE NOOO TIME TO THINK ABOUT A BABY. I ALWAYS DREAMED OF GOING TO HAVARD TO STUDY LAW. ☹ WHAT IF THE TEST IS POSITIVE? I'M GOING TO THE STORE NOW TO BUY A TEST. MOM WOULD NEVER THINK THAT HER LITTLE GIRL WOULD BE HAVING A BABY. MY DAD HAD LEFT HER WHILE I WAS A BABY TO GO TO THE ARMY. HE MARRIED A WOMAN IN ANOTHER COUNTRY AND NEVER RETURNED. I SAW A PICTURE OF HIM. THAT WAS THE LAST TIME MOM AND I EVER SEEN HIM AGAIN.

WHY DO MOST TEENAGERS WANT BABIES?

THERE ARE MANY REASONS WHY TEENAGERS WANT BABIES INCLUDING LOW SELF ESTEEM, NOT ENOUGH PARENT INVOLVEMENT OR LOVE FROM THE ABSENT PARENTS. IN RETURN MANY YOUNG PEOPLE SEEK LOVE AND ATTENTION FROM HAVING A BABY TO LOVE OR CARE FOR VOWING NOT TO LEAVE THEM LIKE THEY WERE LEFT. OTHER REASONS COULD BE TO REBEL AGAINST THEIR PARENTS, TO PROVE THAT THEY ARE GROWN UP ENOUGH TO HANDLE RESPONSIBILITIES, AND IF THEY WERE RAPED TO BE ABLE TO GIVE LIFE FOR ANOTHER PERSON THROUGH ADOPTION. (WE'LL TALK MORE ABOUT ADOPTIONS IN CHAPTER 3.)

FACTORS AT THE ROOT OF TEEN PREGNANCY

I CANNOT SPEAK FOR EVERY TEEN, BUT LIKE I TELL EVERYONE THERE ARE FACTORS AT THE ROOT OF TEEN PREGNANCIES. MANY RESONS WHY TEENS WANT BABIES as I explained BEFORE ARE NOT ROOTS. SOME WAYS TO GET INVOLVED IN THE ROOT FACTORS ARE BY GIVING THE TEEN SOMETHING TO LOOK FORWARD TO OTHER THAN RAISING BABIES AT EARLY AGES. If you have been raped or molested and became pregnant there are some counseling available through your local health department. You can ask God to direct you and your family through the decision of the pregnancy. It can be a difficult thing if you find yourself in a situation where you have a child by someone in the family or molested by a friend. Get counseling immediately and seek authorities do not wait, Let your parent or guardian know quickly if you are getting molested. PARENTAL INVOLVEMENT IN THE CHILD'S FRIENDS, SCHOOL, DATING LIFE, ACTIVITIES, AND COMMUNITY INVOLVEMENT ARE ALL ROOT FACTORS. I too have a teen that even though I trust her, some may say I'm too into her life. Being active in School, friends, and adults she deals with. HOW MANY OF US PARENTS

GET SO TIED UP INTO MAKING A LIVING AND TAKING CARE OF OTHER THINGS THAT WE TRY TO TRUST OUR CHILDREN TO BE WHAT WE THINK THEY ARE NOT. TEENAGERS! MOST OF US KNOW HOW WE WERE AS TEENAGERS AND EXPECT OUR CHILDREN TO HAVE HALOWS. (NO OFFENCE TO ANYONE, REAL TALK REMEMBERS?) A LOT MORE TEENAGERS THAT HAVE BABIES AS TEENAGERS COME FROM SINGLE PARENT HOUSEHOLDS, LOWWER INCOME FAMILIES AND DOMESTIC VIOLENCE/DRUG INVOLVED FAMILIES. THIS IS NOT THE CASE A LOTOF TIME. MORE INFLUENCE COMES FROM TELEVISION, MUSIC, AND THE INTERNET. Some parents have raised teens to be very success and never had to tell them twice about pregnancy. God blessed you. Some parents reminded so much that the teen felt the y had to do something to prove a point. REMEMBER IF YOU ARE A TEEN AND BECOME PREGNANT YOU WOULD HAVE THIS TO LOOK FORWARD TO WHEN YOUR CHILD REACHES YOUR AGE OR WORSE BEFORE!! Something's come back around again and worse! According to the National Center for Health Statistics, Texas leads the country in teen births. Studies show that teen mothers have a high rate of welfare dependency. With little or no training to provide for a child, teen mothers have often had to resort in living with other family members, shelters or even homeless. Some teens are told that it is ok to live with their parents, but from episodes on TV shows. Newly grand-Parents can be left bitter helping to raise their grandchildren with little or no support also. Supportive parents of the pregnant teens are the best way monitor the growth of the teen parenting. Therefore helping with education, child care and other needs of being a parent while still a child. This is good if you have this kind of support. Again most do not. Parents may have other children to tend to have to work or continue with their own lives. Teen shelters and maternity group homes have been established in my home town in Texas to guide young ladies through the process if keeping the child is their option. Some facilities may not have open room available and if you are accepted into the program it involves rules as any place would. If no room is available someone may work with you about foster placement. A lot of teens do not like that idea thus ending up homeless. Some say yes I can just go stay at my friend's house? How long will that last before, tragedy happens? You can stay here for a little while for free but lights, water, food the baby needs for nourishment is growing inside you. Some may let you stay for a while but what if you get mad at them? Or you want things your way? What if you are asked to do something that you know is not right for you or the baby growing inside of you? Teen abuse is a growing factor and many teens are first abused when they get into the relationships AND ARE AWAY FROM PEOPLE WHO CARE .Ask yourself, will you get necessary training and get to go to school? Some people think that having a baby is glory but you have to be prayerful and do things with decency for the protection of not only you anymore, but a child that is growing inside.

1. Will my parents be able to help financially and spiritually if I made the decision to have a baby? _____.

2. Can I honestly rely on friends or people who say they love me to look out for my best interest and the interest of my baby? If so who? (Name at least three responsible people) _____, _____,_____.

3. Do I want to leave home to find out about life only to find out that I had a great life at home? Or is my condition so bad at home that I need to get away with or without a baby? (If your life is endangered get with a local authority member, church member to report abuse, don't look to having a baby a way to get out!

4. Will I be able to go to school or even get a college education, if I decided be a better supporter of my family? Name three occupations you want to do in life to support a family? _____, _____, _____.

5. What college do I dream of attending one day? (Name at least three choices) _____, _____, _____.

6. What activities can I do to keep me from wanting a baby while still a baby? Ex. sports (Name at least three) _____, _____, _____.

7. How can I help friends or family that wants a baby as a teenager chose not to? Ex, encourage adult involvement (name at least three)_____, _____, _____

8. Are the people around me wanting what is best for me and baby, not abusing me all the time? _____.

9. My reaction if I was pregnant?_____
   _____
   _____
   _____
   _____.

10. What would be my Partners reaction to my pregnancy?_____
    _____
    _____

11. Goals for my pregnancy?_____
    _____
    _____
    _____
    _____
    _____
    _____
    _____
    _____
    _____
    _____
    _____

12. Question for my practitioner at my next visit. _____
    _____
    _____
    _____
    _____
    _____
    _____
    _____
    _____
    _____
    _____

CHAPTER 2

SINGLE PARENTHOOD OR TEEN RELATIONSHIP?

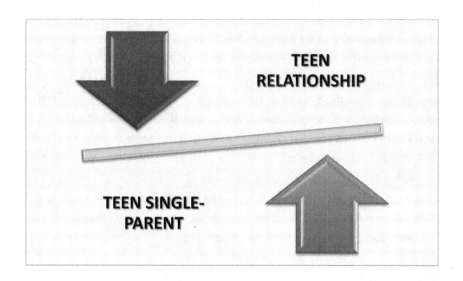

Boys: do not lay down with a person you do not plan to spend the rest of your life with.

The lord said "it is not good for the man to be alone. I will make a helper suitable to him" Gen. 2:8.

Girls: Know his dreams, goals, morals and if they fit your upbringing and family.

The bible says that "Now as the church submits to Christ, so also wives should submit to their husbands in everything." Eps 5:24

COCO'S DIARY ENTRY:

March 22, 2000

Dear diary,

Crystal finally convinced me to take this stupid pregnancy test. I am staring at the two blue lines on the test in shock and confusion. How could I have been so careless is all I am thinking about. Not so much worrying about what mom is going to do to me when I tell her. How could I face anyone like this? I can't stop crying. Now life as I imagined is over and I don't know how I am going to get through this alone. Thinking about Russell and how he is going to college in a few months. Should I just get an abortion and don't tell anyone? Should I keep it a secret from everyone until I start to show? No, I'm a cheerleader, I cannot do that. What about giving the baby to a loving family who will have no problem supporting the baby? What if I just get an abortion no one will know and it's still early. Will God think I am a murder? Did I just knowing make myself to be a single parent? No Russell loves me, he told me time and time that he cares. But he does not want a child. Will he leave me to go to college? I would not want to raise a baby alone without the father being here with me. I want him to get his education so that he can be someone great one day. So much to think about so little time.

Future and a hope

God knows the plans that he has for us. It is to prosper us and give us hope.

Jeremiah 29:11-13 says "for I know the plans that I have for you, declares the lord, "plans to prosper you and not harm you, plans to give you hope and a future. Then you will call upon me and come to pray to me, and I will listen to you. You will seek me and find me when you seek me with all your heart."

Trust that god has a good future for you and whatever choices and decisions you make will be in the will of god. Boys and girls should be aware that whatever you are doing in your life in the present will most likely impact your future. Be aware that your sins are not gone unrecognized by God. Make sure that you do what God wants and everything else will follow.

I know peer pressure is very hard to escape, with so many young adults exposed to explicit music, TV, and bad things on internet. Knowing the background of the person who you are dating and making sure they have the values as your own values, interest and most importantly God. Some of your peers may have been in dangerous family situations or have mental issues that may cause a threat to you if there is a child brought into the scenario. Guys you do not want to be on child support for the rest of your life. Yes, if not paid it will not go away. Sexual intercourse is indeed for marriage and is blessed in the bedroom. I am not stopping you in the ground if you have already started to experiment I am writing from personal experience that it could be hard for you to deal with. It is not wise to sleep around with different girls and guys to satisfy the natural hormone fix that is taking place within your growing bodies. Pleasing others is not what god wants if you are not doing it for God. In reality, having relations with people you are not married to can make god unhappy. God ordained or made sexual relationships for people that are married and he blesses the bedrooms of marriage. Be careful to choose a relationship wisely if you are thinking about dating and within dating age. If you are not at least 16 there should be not room or thoughts of dating. You should be enjoying the time that you have for family, friends and school. If you are older than making that decision could mean spending time outside of family, friends, and school to get to know the other person. This could be time consuming to the goals and dreams you have already in life. Understanding this could allow you the opportunity to follow your dreams and goal before dating or choosing a spouse. Priority is what can make a difference in having a family. Even now with myself I have had to prioritize my life around my children because of things that I thought were more important and now I have children and they come first. Boys it is good to have a wife that you know is pure for you when the time comes and you are ready to give her all of you. For example, have an education and job security so that can support a family and baby. Get the love of god in you so that you can maintain a family through hardships and problems with god grace and mercy. Girls know that when you are giving your body away that god wants what is best for you. Know and trust that it is best to wait for that day when you and your new husband have everything under god will include marriage. The best things are given to those that wait. Remind him that he must wait for a blessing that god has and is preparing for him when the time is right. One day god will allow you to be married in his will. Remember he want you to be submissive to this man or woman. Choose wisely. Please contact the child abuse hotline if you are suffering or in danger at 1-800-4-A-Child (800-422-4453) or contact Child Help at 480-922-8212 and visit the website www.childhelp.org.

Types of STIs and STDs

Gonorrhea, chlamydia, syphilis, Herpes, HIV and AIDS, These are just the main ones. Visit www.cdc.gov for more information. The center for disease control can show you alarming numbers of people in your age group and in your city and county who actually come in for treatment. You will be shocked!!!!!!!!! Don't make yourself part of the statistics. Think about having a baby later and passing an incurable disease to your child! For more information please contact the National AIDS clearinghouse hot line 1-800-342-AIDS, or in Spanish 1-800-344-FIDA.

Birth Control methods:

Abstinence is the most effective, Pills (contain hormones), condoms (Latex and Lambskin), foam (contains nonoxonal 9 spermicide), female condoms, shots and IUD (intrauterine devices). 90% have side effects that are serious and can have lasting effects so read carefully to find the best method for you.

If you think you are still suffering, please contact the National Runaway hotline at 1800-448-4663

PART 2

MAKING A CHOICE: OPTIONS AVAILABLE AND STRATEGIES FOR PARENTING

Stop reading if you think that you have read what you need to know and pass to someone who is pregnant or maybe thinking of becoming pregnant.

Don't take the hard road when the path that is easy becomes clear and you have found understanding.

Yolanda Thibodeaux-Henderson

CHAPTER 3

ADOPTIONS: OPEN, CLOSED, SEMI-OPEN

Every good gift and every perfect gift is from above and comes down from the father of lights–James 1:17

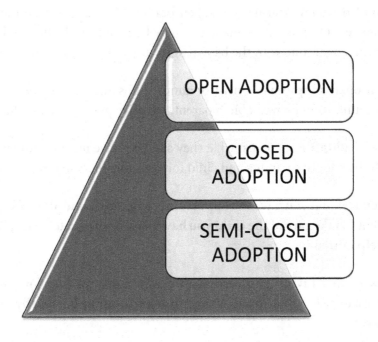

Are you ready to be a parent?

Adoption is a good choice if you have considered it. It may be that you know someone who does want a child .maybe have come to the reality that you will not be able to provide for the child and think this would benefit you and the baby for mom, friends or maybe strangers to adopt the baby. There are three types of adoptions to choose from open, closed or semi- opened. An Adoption Specialist can help you with any method and with telling the birth father about your adoption plan. Whether you want to tell him in person, in a letter or on the phone, your Adoption Specialist can coach you on how best to approach it. Call 1.800.ADOPTION for free info or to speak to a specialist if this is one of your choices.

Open adoptions: are where you know the family who will be taking care of the baby. You have an open line of communication either by phone, email, internet or mail. You may be able to visit the child and have personal time with the baby if agreed.

Semi open adoptions: consist of almost the same except fewer to no communication between birth parent, adoptive parents, and child.

Closed adoptions: are just what they are. You have no communication with the adoptive parents and child for your own personal reasons.

If you feel that you have the opportunity to give life and allow a loving parent to take care of the child you have been impregnated with, there is help available.

Prescreened loving and responsible adults are waiting for you to make a decision that could change your and your unborn baby's lives forever.

Adoption misconceptions and statistics

There are some myths about adoption trouble prospective teen birth parents and adoptive families. For example, the adoptive parents may wonder if they will love an adopted child as much as a biological child; birth parents may worry that their child will have ill feelings toward them. Outside the adoption community, little has been done to change these perceptions.

Recently, the U.S. Department of Health released adoption statistics from a 2007 National Survey of Adoptive Parents. The evidence disputes common misconceptions about adoption, as the adoption statistics prove many widespread misconceptions are false.

General Adoption Misconceptions vs. Adoption Statistics

Misconception: "Will the child that I give up for adoption be cared for?"

Fact: Adoptive families and birth parents ca possible both have this concern before the adoption. Fears of the adoptive family not loving an adopted child are eliminated as soon as they first lay eyes on their baby in nearly every adoption.

Statistics : Adoptive parents interact with adopted children just as well or better than some biological parents, nearly 3 of every 4 adopted children ages 0-5 are read or sung to everyday, while only half of non-adopted children receive the same attention from their biological parents. Furthermore, well more than half of all adopted children eat dinner with their families at least six days per week.

These statistics show how adoptive parents cherish the time they have with their children. They appreciate the opportunity to be a parent every day. Couples with infertility have an astounding appreciation for parenthood. Adoption grants their dreams of raising a child, and their love shows in the little things like reading before bed.

The study says that 9 out of every 10 adoptive couples said the relationship they share with their adopted child is "very close." Nearly half said that the relationship is "better than expected." More than 9 of every 10 adoptive parents said they would "definitely" make the same decision to adopt.

Birth Mother Misconceptions vs. Adoption Statistics

Misconception: " My child or family and friends will hate me more than likely if he or she found out I placed him or her for adoption."

This misconception and fear is maintained by the media and people with no adoption experience. A family member or friend may not be in agreement if a pregnant teens desire to place her child for adoption and may say that the child will hate her if she does so. Some TV shows and movies have unjustly portrayed adoptees this way as well.

Statistics: more than 90 percent of adopted children ages 5 and older have positive feelings about their adoption.

Misconception: "After I place my baby for adoption, I will never see her again."

Fact: At one time, this used to be a true statement. It was thought that the adoption process was easier for everyone if the birth mother went on with her life not knowing anything about her child. However, the past several decades have changed openness in adoption. Now most adoption professionals agree that a semi-open adoption – in which pictures and letters are exchanged through adoption professional mediation after the adoption – creates healthy relationships. Many adoptions are even more open. Keeping some contact with the adoptive family gives the birth mother peace of mind that she made the right decision.

Statistic: 100 percent of birth mothers can choose the amount of openness and involvement in the adoption process and select a family that meets her request. Therefore, 67 percent of private adoptions now have pre-adoption agreements for a semi-open or open adoption.

Myth: "My child won't know or understand that she was adopted."

Fact: Before today, adoption was very "secretive." A birth mother was more ashamed to tell anyone she was pregnant. she would move to another city to place to give the baby up for adoption. In those kind of circumstances, the adopted parents would not tell child that he or she was adopted.

Statistic:99 percent of adopted children ages 5 and older know that they were adopted.

More Adoption Statistics About Birth Mothers

- Women who have chosen adoptions have higher educational goals and dreams. They are also more likely to finish school and are less likely to live in poverty or receive public assistance than mothers who keep their children.
- Women who have chosen adoptions wait to marriage longer are more likely to eventually marry and are less likely to divorce.
- Women who have chosen adoptions are more likely to be employed 12 months after the birth and less likely to repeat out-of-wedlock pregnancies.
- Women who have chosen adoptions are no more likely to suffer negative psychological consequences, such as depression, than are mothers who rear children as single parents.

Adoptive Family myths vs. Adoption Statistics

Myth: "Adopted children are not as healthy as non-adopted children."

Fact: Some worry that a birth mother won't take care of herself during pregnancy if she is placing the baby for adoption and wonder if the child will grow up with poor health.

Statistic: According to The National Centers for Health Statistics, 85 percent of adopted children are rated to have "excellent" or "very good" health while 82 percent of non-adopted children have the same rating.

Myth: "Adoption agencies will not disclose significant medical information about the adoption, birthmother and child."

Fact: State adoption facilities once thought it better to withhold medical records. They thought that the child would have a better chance of being adopted if medical records were withheld, but this practice did more harm than good. After lawsuits and a shift in perception, state governments, private agencies and many state laws and regulations now mandate that all known medical information be disclosed to the adoptive family. This information is extremely important for an adoptive family to watch for health concerns in the adopted child.

Statistics related to General Adoption

- In 2007, 38 percent of children adopted in the U.S. were adopted through private domestic adoption, 37 percent were adopted through foster care and 25 percent were adopted internationally.
- 62 percent of children adopted privately are placed with the adoptive family when they are newborns or less than one year old..
- 88 percent of adoptive parents describe themselves as a "happy" couple, while 83 percent of non-adoptive parents describe themselves as a "happy" couple.

Statistics related to Education

- At American Adoptions, more than 95 percent of adoptive families have a high school education, and more than 90 percent have a bachelor's degree. Nationally, adoptive parents have high school and/or secondary education in 79 percent of private domestic adoptions.
- Adopted children ages 6-11 are just as likely to read leisurely and actively as non-adopted children.
- Children adopted privately are more likely to be involved actively in school than children adopted internationally and through foster care.
- 85 percent of privately adopted children ages 6-17 participate highly in extracurricular activities.

Statistics related to Home and Neighborhood of

- Almost half of privately adopted children are the only child living in the home.
- Adopted children are more likely to live in neighborhoods that are safe, that have amenities and that are in good physical condition than are non-adopted children

CHAPTER 4

TYPES OF ABORTIONS, RISK INVOLVED, AND CONSEQUENCES

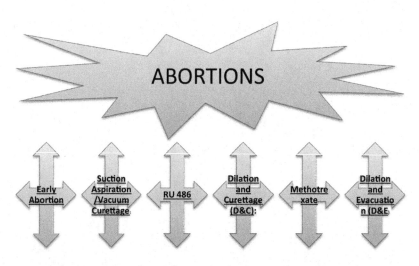

WARNING: THE GIFT OF LIFE COMMUNITY HOME,INC DOES NOT CONDONE ABORTIONS NOR TEEN PREGNANCY WE ARE ONLY HERE TO GIVE YOU THE FACTS AND NOT OUR OWN OPINION ABOUT THE MATTER OF ABORTION.

Yes, sons are a gift from the lord;
the fruit of the womb is a reward.
-Psalms 127:3

If you still cannot decide on a decision for your future after learning about your pregnancy, you may have thought of an abortion. You should keep your options open and keep away from this method. Not because of an opinion that I have, but if you have an abortion you may live with the hunting questions that will never fade. For instance, what gender would the baby have been, and so forth? I have interviewed several other women that have had abortions. They have all had the same hunting questions. That is the reason we have given you the information for adoption. A loving family would love to have the chance to help you in any way to keep the child alive and healthy. We are not here to judge your decision on abortion. We are here to give you risk of them to let you know what you are prone to or capable of happening as a result, just like pregnancy. God has ordain and made provision for the child before forming in the womb so please try not to give your time or energy to this option. Just like there are risk in abortions there are also risk in teen pregnancy so leave them both to the lords timing,

Types of abortions

- **Early Abortion**
- **Suction Aspiration/Vacuum Curettage**
- **Dilation and Curettage (D&C)**
- **RU 486**
- **Methotrexate**
- **Dilation and Evacuation (D&E)**
- **Instillation Methods**
- **Partial-Birth Abortion**
- **Hysterectomy**

RISK – DEATH, MESS WITH THE LINING OF UTERUS, UNABLE TO HAVE CHILDREN IN THE FUTURE, USING AS A FORM OF BIRTH CONTROL-MENTAL TORTURE

Abortion consequences

In a survey taken in the first few weeks after the abortion procedure, between 40 and 60 percent of women questioned reported negative reactions. Within 8 weeks after their abortions, 55% expressed guilt and 31% had regrets about their decision.

For more information about abortions view the website http://www.abortionfacts.com/reardon/after_effects_of_abortion.asp . In another survey of women who were experiencing negative post-abortion reactions, 53% felt forced by others to have the abortion and 95% of these women were not at all satisfied with their choice today.

Please do not take these statistics lightly. Many young women may feel forced to find a quick solution to a difficult situation. There are people who care for you as well as the unborn baby don't let a quick reaction of abortion hunt you for life.

CHAPTER 5

PARENTING PLAN: ESTABLISHING A HEALTHY PARENTING PLAN

COCO'S DIARY ENTRY:

March 24, 2000

Dear diary,

I finally worked the nerve to tell Russell that I was pregnant. I decided to wait until we were alone and I gave him the news. He took it rather hard. I never had seen him cry before. I wondered if he would be mad and dump me when I told him, but he was very understanding of me and the situation. He had asked me if I had told my mom, and I told him that I did not want to tell her until we both had sat down to talk. Crystal had found a brochure of this program that assist teens through pregnancy. The Gift of Life Community Home, INC was the name of the agency. Their mission is to make sure mentoring and options were given in our situation. They even had a place for skills, adoption counseling, and living arrangements. I told him that I thought about keeping the baby since I felt that I could try to get a job after the baby and work extra hard to finish high school. I knew I would have to give up cheerleading and my social life. I felt that even though I made a mistake to have sex before marriage I would live according to heavenly father's guidance from now on. He told me what I expected to hear, that he would be leaving in august for college rather I had the baby or not. He asked if I would wait for him to come home so that we could be a family again. I was happier than ever that he felt that we could still be a family. Now we had to figure out how we were going to tell our parents.

Is parenting a good choice for me? This is the number one question that a lot of teens ask. Parenting is a difficult but an extremely rewarding experience that requires both patience and strength. You will need time to investigate your options and to understand the tasks of raising your child.

Other questions you may be asking yourself … Am I too young? Will my father or mother be supportive? How can I finish school? How can I stay in this job that I just started? Just remember you are in charge of your life. There are many resources available to help you. You might be shocked by the support of parents and friends.

Single Parenthood

Many women make the choice to be a single parent. If you want to stay in school or to continue your career, there is help available through the Nurturing Network 800-866-4666 and *The Gift of Life Community Home INC, are organizations 1-888-959-2093 whose primary concern is for college women and young professionals experiencing an unplanned* pregnancy. The Nurturing Network can help provide you with housing, counseling, medical assistance, child care, financial assistance, educational, and career programs as well as other helpful services. They will help throughout your pregnancy and after the birth of your baby to assist you with meeting your goals.

Sometimes other relatives such as grandparents, aunts, uncles and friends are willing to help you meet the responsibilities of parenthood. Let them know what goals you have set for your future and the future of your child, and don't be afraid to ask for help.

Joint Parenthood

This could be a positive choice for you and the father of your child. Your goals might be easier to accomplish with the daily support of your partner. Two parents creating a loving family environment for their child can be rewarding. Many couples who planned to get married decide to just move up the wedding date.

Do you have a parenting plan available if you have found out that you or your loved one is pregnant? It's never too late to take some time out to evaluate your options without pressure and opinions of others.

PART 3

A POSITIVE TEST RESULT:

HIGH RISK PREGNANCY

CHAPTER 6

FERTILIZATION THE PROCESS OF CONCEPTION

Once you have taken a pregnancy test and the results are positive you have already gone through the process of fertilization. This will usually have taken place 30-15 days prior to your missed period.

- **Ovulation**
- **Hormones Rise**
- **The Egg Travels to the Fallopian Tube**
- **Fertilization**
- **Implantation: Moving to the Uterus**
- **Pregnancy Hormones**

The development stages of pregnancy are called trimesters or three-month periods, because of the distinct changes that occur in each stage. *Please visit the* **International child birth Education Association** *at www. icea.org for more information on stages of labor.*

What is a high-risk pregnancy?

Your pregnancy is called high-risk if you or your baby has an increased chance of a health problem. Many things can put you at high risk. Being called "high-risk" may sound scary. But it's just a way for doctors to make sure that you get special attention during your pregnancy. Your doctor will watch you closely during your pregnancy to find any problems early.

Please visit **The American Academy of Pediatrics** *at 847-434-4000 and visit the website at www.aap.org .*

CHAPTER 7

NATURAL PREGNANCY DIET...

Foods for a healthy baby

When you are pregnant, eat foods that are packed with as much nourishment as possible for you and your growing baby, It is predominantly important to concentrate on foods that contain abundant minerals, such as calcium and iron. Consume as few additives as possible, so eat organic if you can. Going to your local farmers market can help you get local and organic produce. Eating meat is ok if you chose but try to stick with farmed raised, grass fed meats as much as possible. Lunch time is a great time to have a protein rich meal. Chicken contains B vitamins that help the body cope with stress release energy, and form DNA to benefit you and your baby. Sweet potatoes are both nourishing and easy to digest, making them a great food to eat in the evening.

Digestion friendly meals are best in pregnancy since constipation is a high risk symptom. Try to ease your day with smoothies of fresh fruits, flax seeds, and orange juice.

Try these foods in your grocery list;

Apricots-good source of fiber, iron and antioxidants

Papaya-contains enzymes that assist the digestive system.

Orange Juice-Rich in vitamin C and bioflavonoids to help prevent varicose veins

Flaxseeds-Help prevent constipation and a good source of omega-3 fatty acids

Oat Crackers-release carbohydrates slowly to balance blood sugar levels, and easily digested.

Ginger-natures best antinausea remedies, ginger also stimulates digestion

Avocado-Rich source of omega fatty acids, Vitamin K, and fiber.

Coconut- Contains manganese and healthy essential fatty acids

Arugula-Source of folate and antioxidant phytonutrients

Chicken-Source of protein and typtophan to help the body to cope with stress.

Mango-Prebiotic qualities, plus fiber, VitaminsB6 and C

Eggplant-anthocyanins in the skin of the eggplants help brain cell development

Red bell peppers- contains carotenoids for healthy heart and eyes

Sweet potatoes- contains nutrients that act as antioxidants, and are anti-inflammatory and blood-sugar regulating.

Zucchini-Source of B vitamins including folate

Asparagus-great source of folate to prevent and fight birth defects in pregnancy.

Okra- also a great source of folate that enriches the red blood cells, protects the heart, and lowers the risk of birth defects in babies.

Raspberries- a pregnancy aid in the leaf made for tea, great for toning the uterus but only good to drink in the last two months of pregnancy.

Winter Squashes- Supports healthy pregnancy, contains a large amount of folate that prevents neural tube defects in the baby. For more information on foods and healthy recopies contact Dr. Yolanda Henderson at www.yolandahenderson.liveeditauora.com or call 1-888-959-2093 for a health coach In your city and state.

CHAPTER 8

THE FIRST TRIMESTER: THE FIRST 3 MONTHS

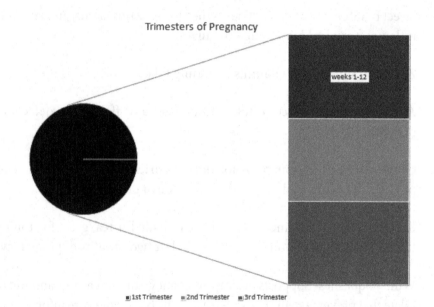

Trimesters of Pregnancy

weeks 1-12

■ 1st Trimester   ■ 2nd Trimester   ■ 3rd Trimester

Monthly Calendar

Month_____

Year_____

Mon	Tue	Wed	Thu	Fri	Sat	Sun

Monthly Calendar

Month _____

Year _____

Mon	Tue	Wed	Thu	Fri	Sat	Sun

Monthly Calendar

Month _____

Year _____

Mon	Tue	Wed	Thu	Fri	Sat	Sun

The first trimester spans from week 1 to week 12 of your pregnancy. You have 3 trimesters in your pregnancy.

If you are newly pregnant or trying to conceive, you have many questions about what to expect. How will your body change? What's happening inside you? Preparing for your nine months of pregnancy so you can be a smarter, more confident, more prepared mom-to-be is wonderful when you choose a holistic pregnancy. Each trimester of your pregnancy is exciting and you have full control which most Doctors don't tell you. It is often a good idea to find a holistic coach and naturopath practitioner. Pregnancy is often the starting point to get most pregnant ladies the habit of using complementary medicine for a variety of conditions. When you are treated holistically, everything about you is important. The practitioner will be looking for the underlying reasons for your pregnancy issues, rather than just the symptoms associated with problems. The most important part of seeing a holistic health Coach is that you are given the sense and power you need to feel in control of your pregnancy and birth processes. By following holistic advice you will gain a deeper understanding of your body, and get a better sense of confidence in your body as a mom- to- be. Let's start with putting it all together. You may just have noticed an absence of your menstruation. After either a home or blood test confirmation. Congratulations! There may be lots of anxiety if it was unplanned, so regain your control, and make the best choices possible for yourself and your baby.

During the first 12 weeks, your body is helping a big group of cells to develop into a fetus with a head, body, limbs, ankles, wrists, fingers and toes. By the end of the 12 weeks this new Baby –2-be will be making its own urine, yet it will only be the size of a thumb. Moms-2-be. Nobody can really even notice that you are pregnant. This is the time that most miscarriages take place so many women do not tell anyone but close relatives or partner of the pregnancy. Moms-2-be may notice fuller and tender breast, frequent urination, moodiness an expanding waistline, feeling of nausea, and vomiting, (morning sickness or throughout the day) and overly tiredness. You may also notice bleeding gums, hair and nails growing faster all because of the increased HCG hormones in the body. Baby-2-Be, is developing at a fast rate, the heart, brain, spinal cord, muscle, and bones are beginning to develop. The placenta, (which nourishes your baby), and the amniotic sac, (which provides a warm and safe environment for baby to move around in). The umbilical cord forms and allows nourishment from mom-to-be to baby-to-be. By the end of the 12 weeks baby 2 be genitals will have formed but you still not be able to see them in an ultrasound. Moms-2-be, now may start to take more care of yourselves, allowing yourself to be pampered and taking a few minutes to relax. For instance, listening to soft music, meditation, and eating a well-balanced diet and eating regularly. Now is not the time to start an extreme workout. Walking and swimming may be your best option to keep fit.

Understanding your pregnancy can help you whether it is increased fatigue, nausea, or cravings to certain foods. Most women experience at least one of these symptoms, those who don't can find it very concerning to the well being of there pregnancies. So embrace all of your symptoms happily and know that there are simple, natural solutions. Let's look at a few first trimester symptoms.

CHAPTER 9

NATURAL PHARMACY

Natural home remedies for
pregnancy symptoms

Needing to urinate more

Is caused by greater volume of body fluids you are producing. Your kidneys are responding by speeding up the process by which it eliminates the waste products. Plus the extra pressure it places on the bladder will increase the situation; they should slow down a bit after the fourth month when the uterus rises into the abdominal cavity. In the meantime try to lean forward when urinating to make sure you are emptying your bladder fully. To avoid night trips to the bathroom, try not to drink a lot 2 hours before bed. Acupuncture, craniosacral work, and osteopathy can all help if the problem becomes really bad.

Nausea/ Morning sickness

Over 80% of most pregnant women suffer with some level of morning sickness. It is believed to be caused by chemical by products of hormonal increase. According to natural baby and mother, get as much rest as you can and make sure you go for walks- the fresh air and exercise will help reduce nausea. If the problem is really bad don't hesitate to talk to your Doctor or Midwife about it. Another great remedy for morning sickness is a slice of fresh ginger (not ginger ale drink, which has no natural ginger) add to a cup of hot water by peeling the skin off the ginger and slicing into little pieces' sip as a spicy tea with raw organic honey.

Tiredness

The body is working in overload the whole pregnancy even while asleep. Be careful not to overdo yourself. Listen to your body. Have a bedtime routine don't do anything that will over stimulate you an hour before bedtime. Evening primrose oil can help counter the effects of tiredness, lavender oil dropped into base oil then added to warm bath water can help make you sleepy. Drink mild herbal teas such as lemon balm or chamomile instead of dinks containing caffeine. Caffeine will make the energy worse. Try getting a relaxing massage, and evening turning on a cd that has your favorite relaxation music or subliminal sleep messages. Good sources of food high in tryptophan could really help in rising of the serotonin levels that are needed for sleep. The foods are almonds, turkey, bananas, almond milk, oats, wheat and local farm raised eggs. Some naturopaths associate iron deficiency with poor sleep so making sure your diet is filled with plenty of dark green leafy vegetables and nuts if you don't eat meat. Keep a sleep diary about the way you sleep and possible any dreams.

Cravings

Very common in pregnancy, but cravings of the wrong type of food (sugars and ice cream) are avoidable if you stick to your healthy diet and not eat too much sugar and fat. Make sure you have a really nutritious diet with fresh organic foods.

FOOD aversions

It is good to go off bad foods like caffeine and alcohol. Most women do, an aversion to healthy foods may indicate a sign of zinc deficiency. Make sure your diet is zinc rich such as meat, nuts, oats, Potatoes, and shellfish if not allergic.

Bleeding gums

Are often the cause of raised levels of the hormone progesterone that softens the gums and increase blood flow. Visit your dentist and use diluted lemon juice as a mouthwash.

Spotty Skin

If instead of glowing complexion, you have acne in pregnancy, there are several natural remedies. Nettle and dandelion teas help to clear the toxins that result in spots. Echinacea is safe to take in pregnancy and will help to avoid the spots from becoming infected. According to Natural mother and baby, calendula cream helps.

Tender Breast

Is not a fun feeling but can be maintained by wearing a well fitted bra and soothing your breast with lavender oil compresses.

Constipation

Slow elimination is from the muscles around your bowel starting to relax. Try not to avoid it because the problem then turns into hemorrhoids. Keep your diet rich in fruit and vegetables, drink plenty of water. Also massage your tummy in a clockwise direction, starting at the left, can help. Also massage your tummy in a clockwise direction, starting at the left, can help. turns into hemorrhoids. Keep your diet rich in fruit and vegetables, drink plenty of water. Also massage your tummy in a clockwise direction, starting at the left, can help.

Headaches

Often caused by hormonal changes, but can also be due to tiredness, stress, and hunger. So, stay rested, stress free and well fed. Also, massaging a drop of lavender essential oil into the temples (sides of the forehead) may help. Yoga may help with headaches by doing gentle stretches applying pressure to bring your ear towards your shoulders. This may help to release tension in your neck that can lead to a headache.

Heartburn

Is often caused by the relaxation of the ring of muscle separating the esophagus from the stomach, this leads to harsh digestive juices going back up the esophagus. It's more likely in pregnancy because there is increased pressure on the stomach, but it can help to eat small frequent meals rather than big irregular ones. Good practice is to chew your food thoroughly and avoid drinking or eating too many acid forming substances like tea, coffee, spicy foods, sugar, cakes, etc. Papaya and pineapple both help with the digestion process, so try eating them daily or you may buy the papaya or pineapple tablets and eating them with a meal. Another good recommendation would be to sip chamomile or lemon balm tea.

Dizziness and fainting

Fainting is often rare but dizziness is common in the first trimester and is due to the pressure on your blood supply to meet your circulatory system, according to Natural mother and baby Keep your blood sugar levels stable with frequent, high –protein meals. Sucking on ginger (crystalized) can help if your dizziness is related to morning sickness. Sipping on lemon balm tea can help or try inhaling lavender essential oil from a tissue.

Herbs while pregnant

Lime flower, passion flower, lemon balm, orange blossom, rose petal or chamomile are safe to use while pregnant. You can add any of them to boiling water and add honey or stevia to sweeten.

Herbs and medications to Avoid

Please avoid taking any medication in pregnancy that is not vital to maintain your health and herbal remedies should be treated with caution According to Natural Mother and Baby. The herbs to avoid are aloes, angelica, barberry, Beth root, black cohosh, bloodroot, buckhorn, cascara, sagrada, catnip, celery seed, cinchona, coltsfoot, cottonroot, elecampane, false unicorn, fenugreek, feverfew, ginseng, gotu kola, goldenseal, greater celandine, holy thistle, hops, horsetail, hyssop, juniper, lady's mantle, liferoot, liquorice, male fern, mandrake, marigold, milk thistle, mint, motherwort, myrrh, pennyroyal, peppermint, poke root, prickly ash, red clover,rhubarb, rosemary, rue, saffron, sage, senna, shepards purse, southernroot, tansy, thuja, uva-ursi vervain, white hourhound, wild indigo, wild yam, wormwood, yarrow and yellow dock.

Essential Oils for aromatherapy

Aromatherapy is one of the oldest forms of medicine, dating back to 6,000 years to ancient Egypt, India, and Persia. They were brought to Europe by crusaders, and by the middle ages they were being used for perfumes and medicines. In France, doctors used essential oils as an alternative to antibiotics and the oils are often chosen by pregnant women who want to avoid traditional medicine. They are a great way for the partner to get involve by mixing oils and giving mom-2-be a massage. They are very easy to use, according to a study of given aromatherapy in labor 54% says they found lavender to be helpful and 64% found frankincense to be beneficial. Please remember that oils are powerful substances and should always be diluted properly and handled with care. The best use of essential oils are 10 drops to 2 teaspoons of carrier oils. (Carrier oils such as sunflower, sweet almond, coconut, or olive oil. Six of the best oils to use are Geranium- Good for backache

Neroli- good for digestion problems

Bergamot- for sadness and depression

Frankincense-(my favorite EO) for stress, aches and pains, skin tone and stretch marks.

Chamomile- for backaches, aches and pains, headaches

Lavender- for backaches, headaches and migraines, muscle and joint pain, insomnia, coughs and colds.

Essential Oils to avoid

These oils are based upon the oil that is known to thin the blood or stimulate the onset of a period should not be used in pregnancy because of the risk. They are: Basil, Hyssop, Parsley, pennyroyal, and sage.

Please visit the American botanical Counsel on their website www. herbalgram.org

Miscarriage

Is called the early termination of birth. One in four pregnancies typically end in miscarriage and are only investigated after the third consecutive miscarriage.

View www.miscarriageassociation.org for more information on miscarriages

CHAPTER 10

THE SECOND TRIMESTER: THE SECOND 3 MONTHS

Trimesters of Pregnancy

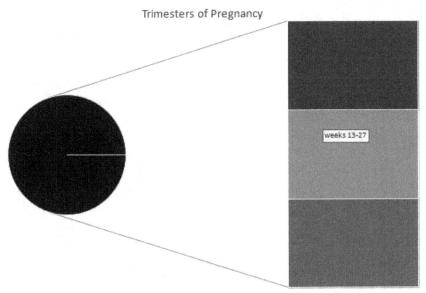

Monthly Calendar

Month _____ Year _____

Mon	Tue	Wed	Thu	Fri	Sat	Sun

Monthly Calendar

Month _____

Year _____

Mon	Tue	Wed	Thu	Fri	Sat	Sun

Monthly Calendar

Month _____

Year _____

Mon	Tue	Wed	Thu	Fri	Sat	Sun

Second trimester

Your second trimester has come and you can breathe again. The second trimester has a reputation for being the 'energetic phase' of pregnancy. This trimester last from week13 to week 28 of your pregnancy. Don't expect to be back to pre-pregnancy energy levels. Don't be ashamed of unexpected attention and belly rubs from strangers. Focus on healthy eating, doctor visits, and exercise. The baby-2-be eyes can now move its eyes. Mom-2-be, will be able to feel the baby kick around the 16th week it's called quickening and feels like butterflies or flutters in your tummy. You can share the baby kicks with your partner to help him feel included in the pregnancy. It is the milestone of your pregnancy if you've been waiting to feel the baby kick. On the other hand, you may feel a little anxiety with the preparedness of a new life and upcoming life changes for both you and baby. By the end of this trimester babyu-2-be will be kicking and jumping a lot especially to loud noises. You may feel a pattern of wakening and sleeping from baby. You will now be able to see the sex of the baby. The weight gain in pregnancy varies but the expected ideal weight gain is normally 24-28lbs which includes the weight of the baby, placenta, amniotic fluid and your own body changes. If you started the pregnancy underweight expect to gain 26-35lbs. If you started the pregnancy overweight expect to gain 15-22lbs. Another side of the symptoms includes the clumsiness and forgetfulness. Forgetting is from the hormonal changes. Making a 'to do' list should help you minimize the frustrations from forgetting. Clumsiness is due to a combination of factors. Loosening joints, water retention and lack of concentration. Some issues that may arise in the second trimester are;

Abdominal pain

The stretching of the abdomen and ligaments some pain is expected. This pain may be sharp or cramping like pain that's most noticeable when you are standing up after sitting or lying down, or when you cough. It's always good idea to mention any abdominal pain to your doctor, practitioner, or midwife. You need to seek emergency help if the pain in consistent or accomplice by other symptoms like fever, bleeding, and vaginal discharge or faintness. Natural remedies for the normal type of abdominal pain incudes drinking chamomile, lemon balm and lime blossom tea.

Backache

Backache is another result of your joints loosening up to prepare you for delivering your baby. Swimming is a good exercise for the back, and the yoga cat posture. It is good for lower back pain. A back massage with St. John Wart oil relieves pain and irritation of the nerve endings. If the pain is persistent, consult an osteopath or reflexologist.

Blood pressure

A normal blood pressure should be 120/80. If this reading goes up to anything above 140/90 you have high blood pressure. This is worrisome in pregnancy and can be a sign of preeclampsia. This can be dangerous to both you and baby 2 be. A supervised course of vitamin c and e tablets in the second trimester can prevent preeclampsia. On the other hand, high blood pressure is not always a sign of preeclampsia. Drinking lots of water, avoiding salt and getting plenty of rest can bring down high blood pressure. Garlic powder tablets have been proven to lower raised blood pressure and there is more evidence that fresh garlic combined with watercress works best. So go ahead and add both to your salads. Fresh Garlic is great for blood pressure, and will keep off colds and infections.

Breathlessness

Mild breathlessness is common in the second trimester, caused by hormonal changes and swelling the capillaries in the respiratory tract and relaxing the muscles of the lungs and bronchial tubes, but severe breathlessness, with rapid breathing and Chest pain is something you should get immediate medical advice on. A warm bath with frankincense oil and meditation can calm breathlessness and anxiety.

Chiliasm

Chiliasm is the darkening of the complexion caused by normal hormonal changes. Foods such as wheat germ, mushrooms, whole grains, and fresh fruits and vegetables is thought to help fight the discoloration.

Diabetes

Is caused by the lack of the hormone insulin, which regulates blood sugar levels. The result is that sugar levels rise and this can raise resulting in problem for mom 2 be and baby2 be. Pregnant moms usually produce extra insulin to cope with the increase. Bitter foods such as green bananas. Bu treatment with insulin may be unavoidable if diet alone cannot control the condition. It is essential to treat diabetes because it can lead to complications for your baby. Yoga can help enhance pancreatic function and improve diabetes and Ayurveda PR actioners.

Legs cramps

Nighttime leg cramps

Perineal pressure, rectal bleeding, swollen feet and ankles, thrush.

A birthing plan

A birthing plan may include information such as:

- How far into labor you would like to remain at home
- Eating or drinking during active birth
- Being out of bed
- Wearing glasses
- The location of your delivery, birthing room labor room
- The pain medications
- Using an IV (intravenous fluid administration)
- Internal and external fetal monitoring
- The use of oxytocin (to start contractions)
- Delivery positions
- Episiotomy
- Cesarean section (surgical delivery through incision) or vaginal birth
- The presence of significant others
- Holding the baby immediately after birth
- Management of breast engorgement(filling of milk after post partum) if you are not breastfeeding
- Circumcision (cutting of male foreskin on penis)
- Rooming in
- Postpartum medication
- Length of hospital stay
- Guardianship for baby in case of death due to complications having baby (living will)
- Insurance information
- Labor method such as Lamaze method and LeBoyer method (see glossary)
- Baby names
- Use of analgesics

Some of these plans may require you finding out your hospitals rules and doctor/practitioners judgments. Remember that these plans can be changed during labor since no one can fully predict how delivery will happen.

CHAPTER 11

THE THIRD TRIMESTER: THE LAST 3MONTHS

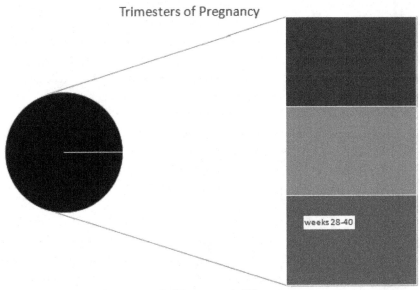

Trimesters of Pregnancy

weeks 28-40

■1st Trimester ■2nd Trimester ■3rd Trimester

Monthly Calendar

Month _____

Year _____

Mon	Tue	Wed	Thu	Fri	Sat	Sun

Monthly Calendar

Month _____

Year _____

Mon	Tue	Wed	Thu	Fri	Sat	Sun

Monthly Calendar

Month _____

Year _____

Mon	Tue	Wed	Thu	Fri	Sat	Sun

Third trimester

This is the last trimester and you can barely see your feet. Congratulations, you have made it this far. You probably cannot walk very strait and seem to be waddling like a duck. You should have everything in order, your birthing plan, baby clothes, suite case, and car seat handy. Soon your belly will be a memory of the past.

Hospital packing checklist

For the labor:

- Your book
- Lip balm
- IPod or music in your cell phone
- Camera
- Lotions or massage oils
- Sugar-less candy
- Heavy socks
- Hair brush / hair tie
- Snacks for labor coach
- Admission forms/ papers
- Health insurance card

_____

_____

_____

_____

For the hospital room:

- A robe and/or night gown
- Perfume or powder to help you feel fresh.
- Toiletries, including shampoo, toothbrush, toothpaste, lotion
- Make up/cosmetics
- Thick Pads (maybe supplied by the hospital)

- Books, cards
- Packs of raisins nuts crackers

Clothing:

- A home going outfit for you remember you will not be back to regular size so maternity clothes are always good still.
- 2-3 maternity bras,
- A home going outfit for baby a stretch suite, t shirt, booties and receiving blanket if it's cold. Hospital will provide diapers.
- Car seat/ carrier (hospitals will not allow you to leave with baby without one. Some hospital provide one for you check to find out)

For Dad or partner:

- Phone
- Camera
- Laptop
- Music
- Stop watch (timing contractions)
- Pillow
- This book
- Snacks
- A gift for baby and mom
- Money for parking or food

Baby Names

Names for a girl   Nickname

_____

_____

_____

Names for a boy   Nickname

_____

_____

_____

Middle names for a girl

_____

_____

_____

Middle names for a boy

_____

_____

_____

Full names (first, middle, Last)

_____

_____

_____

Bleeding during pregnancy cause:

- Pinkish or red streaked mucus appearing soon after exam or intimacy or brownish 24 hours after, is most likely sensitive cervix. This is normal and not a sign of danger. It should be reported to your doctor.
- Bright red bleeding or persistent spotting could be a problem with the placenta and requires quick medical checkup. Go to the hospital immediately.
- Pinkish or brownish-tinged or bloody mucus with contractions or other signs or labor could be the actual start of labor. Go to the hospital immediately.

How to do Kegel exercises

Contract your muscles around your vagina area like you are stopping the flow of urine and hold for ten seconds. Doing these three times a day can prevent episiotomy or a bad tear during labor.

PART 4:

THE STAGES OF LABOR: WHAT TO EXPECT, PREMATURE LABOR & CESAREAN BIRTH

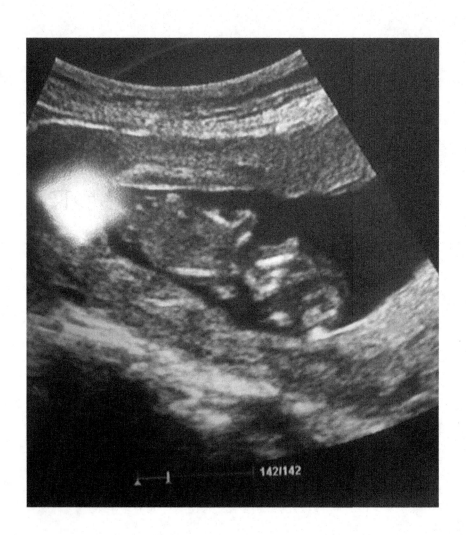

CHAPTER 12

THE FIRST STAGE OF LABOR: CONTRACTIONS

Stages of Labor and Childbirth

Pregnancy labor occurs in three stages and lasts on ordinary 12 to 24 hours for a first birth. Usually, labor is shorter for subsequent births.

The First Stage of Labor

The first stage can last up to 20 hours when dilation of your cervix begins until it's dilated to 10 centimeters. Contractions get stronger when the cervix dilates from 0 to 3-4 centimeters. Minor contractions begin at 15 to 20 minutes apart and last 60 to 90 seconds.

When contractions become only 5 minutes apart, you have entered the Latent Phase. You will soon enter the Active Phase when the cervix dilates from 4 to 8 centimeters; contractions then get stronger at about 3 minutes apart, lasting about 45 seconds. You may have a backache and increased bleeding from your vagina (called the *"bloody show"*). Your mood may switch to a more serious one as you realize delivery will be very soon. This is usually the time you will depend more on your support person.

Breathing and relaxation methods may help. Keep in mind that each contraction is another step closer to getting to hold your bundle of joy.

Upon arriving the hospital, you will be asked to wear a hospital gown then the mandatory checking of yours and the baby's vitals will occur. Your health care provider will also examine your cervix during a pelvic exam to determine how far labor has You may then go over your birthing plan and epidural will be ordered. Most women fear pain and want an epidural. They are very effective at pain relief. Over 90% of women at most hospital receive epidurals. If you have an epidural your pelvic muscle relax and baby will not move with contractions the way it's supposed to. Epidurals can even stop your body from receiving signals to release oxytocin (a hormone that causes contractions) and you may be given Pitocin (artificial oxytocin). You will need to have continuous fetal monitoring, a catheter, and an IV throughout your epidural procedure.

Studies have also shown that babies receive the medications within a few seconds of administering it thus can lead to fussier babies, and disturbance of breast feeding. Please weigh the risk and benefits of epidurals. It is usually the best anesthesia for cesarean. Remember there are risk including paralysis, and getting it too soon could lead to it wearing off before labor begins.

Artificial rupture of the membranes (amniotic sac) may be done by your doctor/practitioner at this time if they have not already ruptured on their own.

Preterm labor

What are the signs of preterm labor?

- Persistent low back pain that feels different what you are used to in this pregnancy.
- Menstrual like cramps
- Intestinal like cramps with or without diarrhea
- Pelvic pressure or tightening that feels different than what you are used to.
- Watery discharge or fluid from your vagina.
- Vaginal bleeding

If labor starts early you should call your doctor/practitioner right away. Once preterm labor has begun it may not be possible to stop the process. You may have to use one or more labor stopping drugs. You will be required to bed rest and complete relaxation to stop reoccurrence of labor as long as possible. You will be given a drug to help the baby's lung develop. If you preterm labor cannot be stopped it is important for you premature infant to be in a neonatal intensive care unit. Premature labor is one that occurs at less than 37 weeks of gestation. Teenagers that become pregnant are very likely to go into preterm labor. On the other hand, all pregnant women are at risk for preterm labor, some are at higher risk than others. Babies born prior to full maturity is the most common cause of infant death or illness. Babies who survive being born too early may have problems gaining weight or growing tall. They may also have problems with vision, hearing, breathing, and coordination. There may also be behavioral or learning problems in these babies as they get older. Most mothers have premature births if they are mal-nutrient, cervical incontinence uterine abnormalities multiple births. *Please visit the* **International child birth Education Association** *at* <u>*www.icea.org*</u> *for more information on stages of labor.*

CHAPTER 13

THE SECOND STAGE OF LABOR: Delivery

The Second Stage of Labor (Delivery)

The second stage of labor begins when your cervix (opening to the vagina) is fully dilated at 10 centimeters. This stage continues until your baby passes through the birth canal, vagina, and is born. This stage may last two hours or longer.

If you have an epidural(intravenous numbing in your spinal cavity), you should not push or you can cause tearing in area between your vagina and rectum without knowing.

Tips to help you push:

- Try many positions: squatting, lying on your side with your leg up, or resting on your hands and knees if possible.
- Take deep breaths in and out before and after each contraction.
- Curl into the push as much as possible; this allows all of your muscles to work.

You may ask if the father can cut the cord. Some birth attendants wait until the cord has stopped pulsating before cutting the cord.

An Apgar scale or score will be taken of your baby in a hospital. The Apgar scale is a test named for Dr. Virginia Apgar, the physician that developed. It will test heart rate, breathing, muscle tone, skin color, and reflex response. A normal score is between 7 and 10 within 5 minutes of birth. Immediate attention is given to a baby with a score of 4 or less. The baby must then be kept warm, and is given to mom in a blanket if score is above 7.

CHAPTER 14

THE THIRD STAGE OF LABOR: DELIVERY OF THE PLACENTA

The third stage of labor begins after the baby is born and ends when the placenta separates from the wall of the uterus and is passed through the vagina. This stage is often called delivery of the "afterbirth" and is the shortest stage of labor. It may last from a few minutes to 20 minutes. You will feel contractions but they will be less painful. If you had an episiotomy or small tear, it will be stitched during this stage of labor.

For more information on stages of labor please visit www.icea.org

Cesarean section

Caesarean surgery or section is not commonly safer than vaginal birth unless there is an health concern. C-sections increase the short term risk of blood clots, stroke, infections, pain, and separation from baby, emergency hysterectomy, and death. the long term risk are pelvis pain, bowel obstruction, infertility, and future pregnancy problems such as ectopic pregnancy, placenta previa (placenta over the cervix), repeat cesarean section and the uterus could rupture.

You may need a caesarean if:

- You are hemorrhaging
- Baby's oxygen supply is blocked
- You have placenta Previa
- Baby is in transverse (lying horizontally across your pelvic) position
- Diabetes
- Pregnancy induced hypertension (high blood pressure)
- Previous cesarean
- Baby is not doing well
- Baby is in breech (head up feet down) position
- Multi-births (twins)

Mothers After delivery care

After your baby is born for the first few hours you will be watched very careful. Your blood pressure and uterus will be checked routinely. Beginning immediately after birth you will produce vaginal flow called lochia. It is a natural way of cleaning and will continue until after the uterus has healed. It will also flow if you have had a caesarean section as well. It will continue to flow heavy like menstrual blood, and could contain clots. Lochia flow showed be watched to make sure it is not too heavy or if it contains clots larger than a lemon.

Most women are very tired after delivery and find rest the best option. Be sure to ask for food if you are hungry even if it's not the normal eating hours at your hospital.

Cesarean after care

If you had a cesarean it would take a lot longer to resume your normal activities. A woman that has had a cesarean will have lost a lot more blood than a normal delivery and could require treatment for anemia. Walking around after could improve circulation and prevent blood clots, reduce intestinal swelling and promote healing.

Hemorrhoids

Hemorrhoids are very common in pregnancy and after delivery. Constipation after delivery can make them worse. You may use medication provided by your hospital for relief of symptoms related to hemorrhoids.

Episiotomy

If mother has had an episiotomy (cut in the perineum) or sutures to repair tearing they may itch and be sore. To relive these symptoms you can:

- Use an ice pack
- Apply cream
- Take sitz baths
- Use hospital provided bottle to squeeze in your perineum area while urinating.
- Sit on a small pillow

Breast care when bottle feeding

If you decide to bottle feed your baby you can ask for medication to dry up your milk. For the first couple of days your breast may be tender and sore to touch. If they get engorged (swollen) apply an ice pack. Do not express milk to relive swelling because this can cause more milk to be produced. Use pain medication for pain and wear a comfortable support bra.

Mothers Hospital stay

The amount of time at the hospital will be determined by different factors: Mother's condition, baby's condition, your personal preference, and the hospital. Many mothers can leave within a day or two of a vaginal delivery. A shorter stay can cost less than a larger one. If you have a caesarean you would have a longer stay on average five days. You can leave sooner or later depending on health outcomes. If the mother leaves earlier a home visit can be arranged to make sure baby and mother are okay.

Labor and Delivery notes

New Mother Experiences

_____

_____

_____

_____

_____

_____

_____

_____

_____

_____

_____

_____

_____

_____

_____

_____

_____

New Father Experiences

_____
_____
_____
_____
_____
_____
_____
_____
_____
_____
_____
_____
_____
_____
_____
_____

PART 5

TAKING CARE OF A NEW BABY: PHYSCIAL, LIFE AND FINACIAL CHANGES

CHAPTER 15

PHYSICAL HEALTH OF THE MOTHER AND CHILD: PROBLEMS AND CONCERNS

There are a lot of physical, financial, and emotional demands of raising a child. Now that you are a new parent or considering parenting, please understand the realities (truths) of it all.

Mom to be, may experience depression or baby blues. If you have the "baby blues" after childbirth, you're not alone-about half of women have a few days of mild depression after having a baby. worrying, a certain amount of insomnia, irritability, tears, overwhelmed feelings, and mood swings are normal. Baby blues usually peak around the fourth postpartum day and subside in less than 2 weeks, when hormonal changes have settled down. But you can have bouts of baby blues throughout your baby's first year. If your depressed feelings have lasted more than 2 weeks, your body isn't recovering from childbirth as expected.

Postpartum depression:

Is a serious medical condition that can be prolonged and disabling without treatment and can affect a baby's development? It is best treated with counseling and an antidepressant medicine. Holistically, dark chocolate with at least 70% cocoa can be beneficial to the mood and provide you with nutrients need. Remember dark chocolate not milk chocolate and usually organic is best. It is bitter in taste but has a happy effect on your mood. It can further improve when you take some home treatment measures. To prevent serious problems for you and your baby, now is the time to work with your doctor to treat your symptoms. If you are having thoughts of hurting yourself, your baby, or anyone else, see your doctor immediately or call 911 for emergency medical care.

Premature Baby:

Pregnancy normally lasts about 40 weeks. A baby born 3 or more weeks early is premature. Babies who are born closer to their due dates tend to have fewer problems than babies born earlier. But even those who are born late preterm (closer to 37 weeks) are at risk for problems.

Why is premature birth a problem?

When a baby is born too early, his or her major organs are not fully formed. This can cause health problems.

Babies who are born closer to 32 weeks (just over 7 months) may not be able to eat, breathe, or stay warm on their own. But after these babies have had time to grow, most of them can leave the hospital. My first daughter was a preemie born 6 weeks early mainly due to me being a teen mother. She only weighed 4lbs 2.8oz, it was by far one of the scariest moments in my life to see her on all the tubes and so small. Thanks to the NICU (neonatal intensive care unit) she was fine and was ready to go home after she was over 5 lbs. 32-3 weeks later.

Babies born earlier than 26 weeks (just under 6 months) are the most likely to have serious problems. If your baby was born very small or sick, you may face hard decisions about treatment.

Jaundice

What is yellow jaundice?

Jaundice is a condition that makes a newborn's skin and the white part of the eyes look yellow. It happens because there is too much bilirubin in the baby's blood (hyperbilirubinemia). Bilirubin is a substance that is made when the body breaks down old red blood cells. If you experience a preemie they will show jaundice and their eyes may turn very yellow and their skin may also be yellow. When you go home pay a lot of attention to their eyes and even had to abstain from giving her breast milk and to switching to formula every so many bottles.

Jaundice usually is not a problem. But in rare cases, too much bilirubin in the blood can cause brain damage (kernicterus). This can lead to hearing loss, intellectual disability, and behavior problems.

In healthy babies, some jaundice almost always appears by 2 to 4 days of age. It usually gets better or goes away on its own within a week or two without causing problems.

In breast-fed babies, mild jaundice sometimes lasts until 10 to 14 days after birth. In some breast-fed babies, it goes away and then comes back. Jaundice may last throughout breast feeding. This isn't usually a problem as long as the baby gets enough milk by being fed at regular times.

Your doctor/ practitioner will probably ask you to keep checking your baby at home to make sure the jaundice is going away. Your baby will need a follow-up exam within the first 5 days after birth. Call your doctor if the yellow color gets brighter after your baby is 3 days old.

What causes jaundice in newborns?

Jaundice occurs because your baby's body has more bilirubin than it can get rid of. Bilirubin is made when the body breaks down old red blood cells. It leaves the body through urine and stool. During pregnancy, your body removes bilirubin from your baby through the placenta. After birth, your baby's body must get rid of the bilirubin on its own.

Breast-fed newborns can become dehydrated easily if feedings are spaced too far apart. This lack of enough milk in the body makes it harder for your baby to get rid of wastes such as bilirubin. Also, some of the things that make up breast milk can change the way the body removes bilirubin.

In rare cases, too much bilirubin may be caused by infections, a problem with the baby's digestive system, or a problem with the mom's and baby's blood types (Rh incompatibility). Your baby may have one of these problems if jaundice appears less than a day after birth.

What are the symptoms?

Jaundice can make your baby's skin and the white part of the baby's eyes look yellow. You may see the yellow color between 1 and 4 days after birth. It shows up first in the baby's face and chest. Babies who have bilirubin levels that are too high may have a high-pitched cry. They also may be sluggish and cranky

Colic

What is colic?

Persistent long periods of tremendous, extreme type of crying in a baby between 3 weeks and 3 months of age is called colic

Doctors usually diagnose colic when a healthy baby cries harder than expected in a "3" pattern: more than 3 hours a day more than 3 days a week for at least 3 weeks in a row. Colic is usually worst when babies are around 6 to 8 weeks of age and goes away on its own between 8 and 14 weeks of age. Colic has been linked but not proven to be from gas. There are a few theories such as an allergy to milk protein or formula, parental anxiety, an immature gastrointestinal tract and nervous system.

It is common to feel scared, upset, or frustrated when you cannot get your baby to stop crying. But remember that colic is normal and temporary. Your baby will grow out of it.

To learn more about colic read Roundtree, Walter, Zand. **Smart Medicine for a Healthier Child***. New York: Penguin Group Second Edition, 2003*

Home Treatment

You may prevent some crying episodes related to colic by developing a strong emotional bond with your baby, which helps both of you to feel more secure and calm. After your baby has started to cry, use comforting and soothing techniques to try to shorten the episode or decrease its intensity. Certain preventive measures may also help. Colic gradually goes away on its own, regardless of what you do. Abdominal messages are good to help baby relieve intestinal problems. Also, try the bicycle exercise techniques which are bicycling your baby's legs in a pedaling motion. Practice this technique several time a day.

*For more information on infant message contact the **International Association of Infant Message** 805-644-7699 and visit them on the web www.iaim-us.com for training, education, and research into the benefits of massage for infants and babies.*

Nutritional Supplements

Lactobacillus Acidophilus (probiotics) taken by the breastfeeding mother to help with friendly bacterial flora in the intestine (stomach)

Lactobacillus bifidus (probiotic) is another great bacteria that helps to improve digestion a bottle-fed baby should take 1/8 teaspoon powder dissolved in milk /formula twice a day.

Herbal treatments

A nursing mother can drink ginger tea, chamomile tea, peppermint tea, and fennel.

We also recommend giving babies tea. Contact our live support at 1888-959-2093 for more information and dosages for alternative treatments; acupressure, herbal treatments, homeopathy and more.

Also, be careful about acting impulsively or using desperate measures to treat colic.

For example, do not:

- Let your baby stay in the crib and cry until he or she is exhausted.
- Stop breast-feeding your baby. This will not cure colic.
- Give your baby aspirin or aspirin products, because of the risk for Reye syndrome.
- Give your baby alcohol (even a pacifier dipped in brandy or other alcoholic beverages).

- Shake or spank your baby for crying. Serious or even fatal brain injuries may result (shaken baby syndrome).
- Give your baby medicine unless it is recommended or prescribed by your doctor.

Some doctors prescribe probiotics, which are bacteria that help maintain the natural balance of organisms (microflora) in the intestines. Studies are being done to find out how helpful probiotics are for babies who have colic.

Self-care

It is important to take care of yourself and remember that colic is not caused by poor parenting. Colic is temporary, and it will not affect a baby's general health or future development.

If nothing seems to console your baby, keep trying comforting techniques, but realize that sometimes nothing works. If you are not successful and you become exhausted by these efforts, ask for someone else to take over for you.

SIDS

What is sudden infant death syndrome (SIDS)?

What causes SIDS?

Doctors don't know what causes SIDS. It seems to happen more often in premature and low-birth-weight babies. It also is seen more often in babies whose mothers didn't get medical care during the pregnancy and in babies whose mothers smoke. SIDS may also be more likely in babies who were part of a multiple pregnancy (for example, twins or triplets) or whose mothers are younger than 20.

When babies sleep on their bellies, they may not breathe well. Not too long ago, side sleeping was said to be okay. But babies placed on their sides can easily roll onto their bellies and could have trouble breathing.

Researchers are studying the possibility that SIDS may be caused by problems with how well the brain controls breathing, heart rate and rhythm, and temperature during the first few months of life. More research on this is needed.

For more information on SIDS please visit the National Healthy Mothers, Healthy Babies Coalition at 703-836-6110 or www.hmhb.org

Down syndrome

Down syndrome also known as trisomy 21 (caused by an extra copy of the 21st chromosome) is a chromosome abnormality that causes mental retardation and physical malformation in babies. It occurs in about 1 in 750 births and increases the chances with age. Amniocentesis can detect this if blood samples are abnormal.

Babies with Down syndrome will require more assistance and help than regular babies and some may die after birth.

Pregnancy loss

The majority of pregnancies are successful for most but some are not. Please do not dwell on the thought that something can go wrong but keep in mind you must take care of yourself during pregnancy.

If a pregnancy loss occurs it is suggested that parents grieve the loss of their child the way any other family member would. You can give the baby a name and have a religious ceremony for the baby. At a hospital you can request for a Chaplin for prayer if you want a memorial for the baby. If the baby is fully formed the parents should see and hold the baby. This may help the feelings of regret later. The mother may have to remain in the hospital but it is suggested that she be moved to another part of the hospital for monitoring to not get depressed by watching other mothers enjoying their babies. Parents may find relief in support groups in your area who have lost a child. If not you may contact SHARE, a clearinghouse for support groups for those who experienced a loss of a child by either miscarriage or still birth at (314) 947-6164.

Twins

Twins about occur about 1in 90 births. Identical twins are formed from a single fertilized ovium that splits completely very early in pregnancy developing into two eggs. They share the same sex, blood type, appearance, and other inherited traits. Fraternal twins are not the same as identical and came be alike or as different as two children of the same parent.

You may experience more discomfort carrying twins than a mother with a single birth and require bed rest in your last trimester for risk of premature birth. A doctor/practitioner will be able to detect two heart beats that could confirm multiple births, usually of your uterus is growing quicker than the norm.

CHAPTER 16

LIFE CHANGES: STRESS AND MOOD DISORDERS

There are a lot of social problems that come after having children. For example, you used to play your favorite sport or cheer on the cheerleading squad without having to think about a baby-sitter. You might have been able to go to the mall with your friends and participate with other important activities. These social changes can result in major depression from stress and other mood and social disorders. Some mood and social disorders in teen parents can result in improper treatment or handling of your child (not limited to dealing with abusive teen relationships). Some important conditions are bipolar, depression (manic and post-partum), social anxiety, and Drug abuse. Manic behavior by a teen with bipolar disorder may result in such problems as:

- Suspension from school.
- Arrest as a result of fighting or drug use.
- An unwanted pregnancy.
- A sexually transmitted infection (STI) from unsafe sexual behavior.

During depressive episodes, a teen may do poorly in school and may stop participating in activities he or she enjoyed in the past, such as a sports team. The teen may even drop out of school to work to support the child.

Watch for warning signs of suicide and teen abuse, which can include preoccupation with death or suicide or a recent breakup of a relationship. Mainly this can occur in young men who are now teen fathers but also in young mothers. The responsibility of having a child can be more than they can handle and cause an alarm in their developing minds.

Substance abuse is common. The teen's doctor may recommend an evaluation for both substance abuse problems and bipolar disorders if the teen appears to suffer from either condition. Please seek help from a Doctor immediately if you or someone you know may have signs of these behaviors. Untreated mood and social behaviors can result in Child Protective Services legally removing your child from your home or possession.

Treating other conditions

Sometimes treatment for other conditions can make bipolar disorder worse. I highly recommend no medications but natural food and supplements.

For example;

- Oats- soothes the nerves because they contain the alkaloid gramine, a natural sedative, which can treat depression, anxiety, and insomnia without side effects. Tea made out of oat straw is a traditional remedy for anxiety and insomnia.
- Walnuts-contain serotonin, a brain chemical that can lift depression.
- St John worts- herbal supplements that lifts depression. It can help treat mild to moderate depression but not severe depression. Studies have shown it to work as well as conventional antidepressants. A great remedy for seasonal, pms and menopausal depression and anxiety.
- Dark Chocolate cococa- Natural raw dark chocolate that contains at least 75% COCOA is a great antidepressant because it contains serotonin, dopamine, phenylethylamine, which are neurotransmitters alleviate depression and well-being.

Dark chocolate contains monoamine oxidase inhibitors (MAO inhibitors) which helps improve our mood. Cocoa contains anandamide which stimulates blissful feelings. It contains B vitamins for healthy brain health.

Treating depression with synthetic antidepressants can trigger a manic episode or make one worse.

Treating attention deficit hyperactivity disorder (ADHD) with stimulants may also trigger severe mania, depression, and even psychosis (loss of touch with reality).

Treatment with corticosteroids for conditions such as asthma may also trigger a manic or depressive episode.

Medicines that intensify bipolar symptoms may need to be stopped or changed to a different dose or medicine. Sometimes an additional medicine (such as a mood stabilizer) can solve the problem. But each teen responds to medicines differently. And it may take several tries before your doctor can identify an effective medicine or combination of medicines for your child's conditions.

Joy and confidence

Joy and confidence is a major need before, during, and after a pregnancy.

Always remember to take time to have a fun and relaxing adventure for the day. This could include walking in the park, going to a movie, or having company with a positive friend or family member. Drink a cup of tea at your favorite park, go dancing at the high school dance, invite a friend over to study. The level of joy depends on you not anyone else so make sure to get plenty. Joy could be taking care of your new baby but you must remember to take time for yourself if necessary. Try using a journal each day to write about your joyful experiences. Include in your journal what you did for the day using these words:

- **Mood**
- **What you appreciate about yourself**
- **Loving thoughts**
- **Prayer and meditation**
- **Visualizing your future**
- **Time to yourself**
- **Meaningful connections with others/relationships with others**
- **Physical activity**
- **What you loved about work/school**
- **Fresh air**
- **Daily goals and steps to your goals**
- **Healthy foods you added**

Usually writing about these things can keep you in a good and positive mood and boost your confidence and how you look at yourself. At the end of every week, go back and reflect on your writings. So many teens are often embarrassed that they have gotten pregnant or ashamed. Get back up again and experience life. It's not over!

CHAPTER 17

FINACIAL:
RETURNING TO SCHOOL
AND BUDGETING PLAN

Trying to adjust to going back to school is also hard and requires planning. Your planning may require finding a decent sitter or childcare while going back to school and or work. Having all of these plans together before deciding to have a child is far better than waiting until after. This may cause a lot of stress and anxiety about finishing your education. A lot of programs are set in place for single parent and teens for childcare depending on your state. *Check with your local workforce Commission or state welfare agency for more information on assistance programs or call us @1888-959-2093.* Also know that if you request state assistance, a paternity test will need to be done. This allows fathers to know if the child is their baby as well. In most states if the paternity test is positive the father has to repay the state for the test. Teen fathers are held responsible to the baby through adulthood. If the teen father is not married to the mother the baby may not continue with his last name if the mother does not choose to. At the hospital is where the baby is named and papers are given for paternity establishment. Fathers can also pay for the paternity test at an outside laboratory in your county. Ask about the local lab information from the social worker at the hospital if you have concerns about paternity. The cost usually varies between 100-200 dollars. If the teens decide to get married you would have to get consent. Check with local laws in your state.

What to look for when deciding on a child care center. You may want to visit a couple in your area with this checklist.

Checklist for childcare centers:

- Is the license displayed in a visible location? Yes No
- Are separate spaces available for the different age groups? Yes No
- Is the quantity of toys and materials sufficient for the number of children in the classroom? Yes No
- Are the toys and materials developmentally appropriate for the different age groups? Yes No
- Is the classroom arranged in a way that toys and materials are accessible to children? Yes No
- Are the furnishings in the classrooms child sized? Yes No

- Are there obvious hazards such as dangerous substances, electrical cords, uncovered electrical outlets, cleaning materials, or medications accessible to the children? Yes No
- Are fire extinguishers on site? Yes No
- Are fire escape plans/emergency evacuation plans posted? Yes No
- Are the sinks and bathroom stocked with appropriate supplies? Yes No

NOT Required by the State

- Is your initial reaction upon entering the child care center a positive one? Yes No
- Is there space for active play and other space available where quiet play may take place? Yes No

Tour of the Center: The Outside

Required by the State

- Do the children have an opportunity to play outside each day? Yes No
- Is the outside area free of litter and obvious hazards such as broken glass? Yes No
- Are there a variety of outside equipment/toys available and appropriate for various ages? Yes No
- Is the outdoor play equipment sturdy and in good repair? Yes No
- Are children being supervised by the child care provider? Yes No
- Is there shade available outside where the children play? Yes No
- Do children two years and younger play separately from the older children? Yes No

NOT Required by the State

- Are the child care providers interacting with the children? Yes No
- Does the center encourage use of the outside area for learning activities as well as free play? Yes No

Interaction Between Staff /Children/Parents

- Is the schedule of daily activities posted and current? Yes No
- Does there seem to be enough caregivers for the number of children in the room? (You may need to ask about staff/child ratios) Yes No
- Are the activities observed appropriate for the ages of the children involved? Yes No
- Do the child care providers follow hand washing procedures after Diapering/toileting? Yes No

NOT Required by the State

- Are children allowed to make choices throughout the day? Yes No
- Do the children seem occupied and engaged by their activities? Yes No
- Are the child care providers handling conflict among the children in a positive manner? Yes No
- Do the child care providers seem patient and receptive to the needs of children? Yes No
- Is there a daily method of communication between the child care providers and parents? Yes No
- If you were a child, would you want to spend your day at this center? Yes No

Operational/Policy Question

Required by the State

- Does the center encourage parents to drop in and visit at any time? Yes No
- Does the facility serve nutritious meals/snacks? Yes No
- Was there a current weekly menu posted in a visible location? Yes No

NOT Required by the State

- Are parents encouraged to participate and be involved? Yes No
- Does the facility enroll children with special needs? Yes No

- Are there child care providers with additional training for special needs children? Yes No
- Does the center participate in the subsidized child care program? Yes No
- Do the hours of operation and holiday schedule accommodate your schools/work schedule? Yes No
- Does the facility charge when a child is out sick or on vacation? Yes No
- Is there a late pick-up fee charge? Yes No
- Does the cost of care include meals and snacks? Yes No
- Does the facility offer transportation? Yes No
- Do ALL staff have current CPR and First Aid certification? Yes No

Additional Questions to Ask:

Not Required By the State

- How much TV are the children allowed to watch?
- How are children disciplined? Are you comfortable with the discipline methods?
- How are nap times handled?
- What kind of security measures are in place to assure the safety of the children?
- What is the center's policy for sick child care?
- What is the center's policy for administering medications?
- Are there any additional activities (e.g. music, dance) available and are costs included in the weekly fee?
- What are the program's staffs to child ratios?
- Do any employees on staff have degrees in Child Development/ Education?

Family budgeting

Now, that you are a teen mother or considering becoming one. You would need to have a budget. You now have a little one to buy for. Clothes, shoes, diapers, food, wipes, more diapers.

This is not a must but only makes life easier if you use it and learn how to use it.

Here is a sample that may be helpful.

Child care	School	Work	Financial	Resources

Couponing may also help. Check with coupons.com or search for coupons for your local stores on the web or in the mail.

Checking and savings accounts are a good way to save for a rainy day. Most banks can open a minor savings account or checking account in your name. Call your local banks for more information. You should have a goal to save at least 10% of your earnings or allowance. For example, you make 100 $ per week in allowance save 10$ per week. That is 520$ per year.

PART 6

HOME MAKING: MAKING A HOUSE A HOME

CHAPTER 18

FEEDING AND BABY HYGIENE

Now that you understand you have to plan your life now around your new addition to your family here are a few pointers to help.

Cooking/ Feeding

The baby maybe breast feed for the first year or so depending on your desire to continue and your schedule permitting. You have a choice of different types of milk if you do not breast feed. They are powder formula, concentrated formula and ready to feed formula (I do not recommend a lot of GMO formula because of the ingredients found in them). Use your best judgment and find organic formula or breastfeed. Please If you receive assistance through your states nutrient program, they may have a special type you may purchase unless prescribed by your baby's doctor/practitioner. Babies usually drink 4oz every 4 hours some babies require more or less pay attention your baby for clues of finishing a bottle if formula remains. You may have to wake the baby to feed if the baby is still sleep but will usually cry for feeding. Be sure to have a warm bottle ready at that time to avoid crying. You can warm babies bottles in a bottle warmer bought at a local baby store or request one for a baby shower gift. Bottles should never be warmed in a microwave since the milk inside maybe hotter than you test. Always test bottles before feeding on your arm. Babies should be held during feeding. After about 6 months your baby starts eating foods maybe even as early as 3 months. I have even heard and given baby cereal in a feeding bottle to thicken the milk. (Warning this could cause constipation) I know grandmas remedy to fatten up the baby may work but spoon feeding your baby solids is the best way. Your baby might spit out some of the food first before learning how to swallow it. Always make sure the bottles are not propped up while lying down this could cause your little one to choke. Milk can even run into the ears giving your baby an ear infection. **If you insist on cereal in the bottle, give milk from a non-cereal regular bottle to help make sure you are providing enough fluid between cereal feedings**. Do not over feed the baby, he/she may choke or spit up. Clean the babies' gums with a wash cloth to prevent milk accumulation in mouth and gums.

- Never prop a bottle or leave baby alone with a bottle
- Do not microwave baby bottle
- Never attach a pacifier around the baby's neck
- Shake or stir all bottles and food before giving to baby

Breast feeding Ladies: If you are breast feeding remember to eat a balanced diet meal three times of day healthy snacks, with plenty of water. You can increase your milk supply naturally by purchasing fenugreek tablets from most food stores. It is helpful to use a weekly planner to help with meal planning for yourself. Have a loved one (Baby's father) or friend to prepare meals for you on a Saturday or get some stir fry vegetable dinners you can quickly reheat. This helps you and the baby. Remember what you put inside your body your baby will also drink through your milk. Keep milk that you pump labeled inside of your freezer marked with date and time if you pump while away. Your milk will leak or let down when nursing time. Remember to take time to rest before returning to hard task. Your body has just gone through a lot of physical torment during the delivery process. Stay in the house unless you have to go out for at least 4 weeks.

Benefits to mom

- Breastfeeding relaxes you-relaxing hormones are released which can calm you
- Breastfeeding saves money by reducing or eliminating the cost of buying formula
- Breastfeeding reduces health care costs.
- Breastfeeding is convenient – no mixing or measuring
- Breastfeeding burns extra calories, so it makes it easier to lose the punds gained during pregnancy.
- Breast feeding helps the uterus to get back to its original size and lessens any bleeding you may have after giving birth.
- Breastfeeding can help you bond with your baby
- Breastfeeding is associated with decreased risk of breast cancer, heart disease, osteoporosis, and depression.

Benefits to baby

- Breast fed babies have a healthier start in life, contains all the nutrients baby needs, regardless of premature or full term.
- Breast milk has the perfect mix of nutrients for your baby digestive system
- Breast milk protects a baby from many illnesses such as diarrhea, ear infections, respiratory tract infections, diabetes, urinary tract infections, and severe bacterial infections.
- Breast milk is always the right temperature for your baby.
- Breast fed babies are less likely to become overweight.
- Breast feeding promotes the proper development of jaw and facial structures
- Breast milk aids in the development of baby's brain and nervous system.
- Breastfeeding is associated with decreased risk of chronic conditions such as obesity and diabetes.
- Some studies even indicate that most breastfed babies have higher IQs than formula fed babies

It is not recommended to breast feed if you:

- Smoke
- Drink alcohol or too much caffeinated sodas
- Infected with serious medical conditions such as AIDS
- Abuse drugs
- Take prescription medications that can pass through breast milk and can be harmful for baby check with your doctor.

Nursing supplies

- Nursing bras-support breast and make feeding convenient
- Nursing pads-pads placed inside of the bra to protect your bra
- Nursing shirts-makes nursing invisible to the public
- Pumps- electric or handheld
- Bottles or feeding bags- storage for milk

Storage of breast milk

- All milk should be dated
- Bottles must always be cleaned
- May be saved in hard-sided plastic or glass containers with well fitted tops or in freezer milk bags designed for storage of human milk
- Breast milk may be stored:
  - o   At room temperature for up to six hours
  - o   In an ice chest/cooler with frozen gel packs for up to 24 hours
  - o   In a refrigerator for up to 8 days
  - o   In a freezer compartment inside a refrigerator for up to 2 weeks
  - o   In a freezer compartment with a separate door for 6 months
  - o   In a separate deep freeze for up to 12 months
- When using frozen milk, you should always defrost in refrigerator. Thaw milk can be safely kept in the refrigerator but must be used within 24 hours. Freeze milk in small quantities to avoid waste.
- Thawing containers
  - o   Never use microwave to thaw breast milk
  - o   Thawing should take place under warm water

For painful breast feeding

- Gentle breast rubs will express milk
- Warm packs
- Breast feeding frequent 8-12 feeding per 24 hours every 1-3 hours
- Start on the least sore side
- Cold compresses to your breast immediately after to prevent swelling.

Goat milk formula Is an alternative milk if you don't want conventional milk or alternate while breastfeeding, most times you would need to add your own vitamins supplements to include in this milk. You can buy the it already mixed or mix it with half parts distilled water. Now, some stores even have Non-GMO formulas if you wish to formula feed without the chemicals inside of most or some formula. *For more information on Support of breastfeeding please contact the LaLeche League International at 847-519-7730 and visit their website at www.lalecheleague.org .*

Laundry

Cleaning your new baby's laundry is not the same as cleaning your own. There is a special kind of soap that is made especially for babies check with your store's baby detergent.

Bathing/diapering

Sponge bath your baby with a wash cloth until the umbilical stump falls off. Be sure the umbilical stump does not get wet with water during sponge baths it can cause the healing process to be prolonged. Use the alcohol pads from the hospital or pour a small about onto a towel and wipe the stump gently.

Your baby's first bath maybe the most fun you will have. Use a gentle soap made for babies to wash the baby's body. You can clean your baby making sure the temperature is not too hot for baby in baby tubs. Always check the temperature by using your elbow (your hands maybe use to hot water and be too hot for baby) some use baby water thermometers to check temperatures. Never leave child unattended in baby tubs! Diapers come in all sizes get sizes according to weight of baby. I actually bought newborn diapers and one of my children was already too large for them by the time he was born. First poop is usually yellowish in color is you breast feed do not be alarmed. It may be black and thick this is normal. You may have to change diapers anywhere from 10-15 per day. **Ladies**: be sure you bath/shower daily especially if you are breast feeding to prevent infections around your nipples and vaginal area. Cloth diapers can be bought and used instead of disposable diapers. They are less expensive but you would have to wash them out to reuse them.

Infants Temperature

The most accurate way to take a child's temperature is to use a digital thermometer rectally or orally. Rectal temperatures provide the best readings for infants," reports the Mayo Clinic. Place your infant on her back and lift her legs. For infants up to 3 months, lubricate the tip of a rectal digital thermometer and insert it 1/2 to 1 inch into baby's rectum.

It should slide in easily, but if you feel any resistance, stop. Hold it in place until the thermometer beeps or otherwise signals that it is done. Remove it gently and check the display. An infant up to 3 months old has a normal body temperature range of 97 to 100.4 degrees Fahrenheit, 36 to 38 degrees Celsius, according to the American Academy of Pediatrics. Temperatures both higher and lower than this range are a cause for concern.

Doctors/Practitioners visits

Be sure to follow up and keep record of all doctors' checkups for yourself (ladies) and baby. Keeping your baby up to date is very important to prevent illnesses. Remember to keep a baby thermometer around if baby starts to feel extra warm. Always check the temperature of a baby in the rectum. Regular temperatures of babies are 97 to 100.4 degrees Fahrenheit. **Ladies** : You may bleed for about 4-6 weeks. Make sure you follow your doctor/practitioners orders to abstain from sexual intercourse until your post-partum checkup. You can get pregnant again if you do not listen.

For more holistic information contact Dr. Yolanda Henderson @ 1-888-959-2093 or visit her on the web at www.yolandahenderson. liveeditaurora.com

Car seat Safety

- Infant should be in a properly installed, safety approved car seat when vehicle is moving never in your arms
- Never place a rear facing seat in the front seat
- Infants must ride in the back seat facing the rear until at least one year of age
- Have a certified passenger safety technician check your car seat installation.

For more information on car seat safety contact the National Highway Traffic Safety Administration at www.nhtsa.dot.gov or call 1888-DASH-2-DOT for information about child safety seats, recalls, and child passenger safety and auto safety guidelines in your state.

CHAPTER 19

ORGANIZING: DAILY PLANNER

Daily planning

It is always good to keep a planner or journal that you can write updates, appointments, and concerns in. Keep in mind that being organized is not only good for you but also for baby. A baby cannot talk so you must be mentally prepared for the extra work involved and being unorganized can make your life stressful. Time management for activities such as school, work if you are old enough, chores, and baby are important in your daily life. Don't forget to ask for help so that you get a chance to take time for yourself. Having an extra task can be a bit rough so be sure to have a responsible person look after your baby for an hour or so. This can help if baby's sleep pattern is different and up in the middle of the night for feeding.

School

If you are not finished with school you may have to adjust the time you have for your baby. You may be filled up with make-up work to catch up on. Do not be afraid to ask for help from a loved one or friend to help you with the baby while you catch up. You might have to adjust your schedule or graduation plans to work towards getting a GED if you do not have proper support. Whatever you do, make that your last resort do not drop out. Some states have schools who can accommodate your needs so that you can still graduate with your class. I am a witness to that, you still can make it do not give up. If you breast feed you are allowed to go to the school nurse to express milk.

Work

If you are under the age of 16 you may not permitted by law to work for wages in your state.

If this is your case you would have to rely on parental support or government support. This may cause you to feel ashamed since you are now put into an adult role while you are technically still a baby yourself. Please keep in mind that you need the adult to help you maintain yourself and baby. Do not try to do this alone or run away from the situation. If you were molested let someone you know and trust immediately. (talk to a friend, doctor/practitioner, teacher). You and your child may be removed from the situation if it is not stable for you or the baby.

If you are over the age of 16 you may be permitted to work and drive in your state.

This gives you a lot more responsibility to achieve things for your new baby financially. When you first begin to work, you may choose a job that is not related to your desired career. If you can for instance, work at a hospital if you desire to be a nurse. Or work in a daycare center if you would like to become a daycare center director one day. Aligning your life with prerequisites in work and school can be very rewarding and keep you on a path you should be on in life.

Working outside and going to school can be hard as well because you are away from baby. Even grown working mothers and fathers find this hard because they miss their children while they are trying to provide for their child.

Make sure to set aside time frames to visit and bond with your new baby whenever and whatever your work/school schedule permits. Don't forget to talk with the employer about breast feeding areas and breaks, if you breast feed and need to pump milk. Bring your ice pack, bottle and pump in a refrigerated area to store until you get home.

HOLISTIC DAILY PLANNER   DATE_____

Morning
Thoughts

Order our Holistic journal by calling 1-888-959-2093 or print several copies before writing

_____

Dreams,
Affirmations,
Intentions

I am grateful for   _____

	Breakfast	Lunch	Dinner

Healthy Food choices

Actions to complete goals example

1._____

   _____

2._____

   _____

Prayer/mediation

Water

Sunshine

Healthy diet

Journal

Exercise

Holistic Activities	Daily Goals		Actions to complete Goals

Rest

Hobby/creativity

Love

Vitamins

Education

Finances

Holistic Activities	Daily Goals		Actions to complete Goals

Spiritual
meditation/prayer

Social activites

Exercise

Healthy
Relationships

Joyfulness

115

CHAPTER 20

SPIRITUAL MEDITATION

A baby is God's opinion that the world should go on.
-Carol Sandburg

PRAYER

SPIRITUAL MEDITATION:

God knows if you are reading this far that you may have made some mistakes in the past. He allowed you to make it through rape, child birth, mental illnesses, bad relationships, STDs, or other bad choices. You probably feel as though you have it so hard right now that you want to kill yourself or do something to harm someone else. Remember troubles don't last always. You have the opportunity to tell him thank you in this chapter of meditation. Remember that he is always with you no matter what the situation is. Your faith to know that God wants the best for all of us and will use a rock, a book, a song, an author, an angel, to let you know that he loves us all. Life is tough enough with the peer pressure and dilemmas we all must face in life with adding additional struggles. Rest assured that he knows every move we make and counted every hair on our bodies he will be there for us in the end. When friends or family let us down, we have him. My recommendation is to get into a bible based church and let God's mercy and favor rest upon your life as a child of God. If you have not accepted Christ into your life, you have the opportunity wherever you are as you are.

Use the space below to write a thank you letter to God.

Dear God, Thank You For _____

_____

_____

_____

_____

_____

_____

_____

_____

_____

_____

_____

_____

_____

_____

_____

_____

_____

_____

_____

_____

For more information on Holistic health and wellness or a spiritual prayer partner contact The holistic Society at www.yolandahenderson. liveeditaurora.com or www.thegiftoflifecommunityhome.wordpress. com and by calling 1-888-959-2093 and to schedule an appointment with a doctor or healthcoach 1-866-267-4576.

Prenatal/Post-Partum Appointments

Date/Time_____Doctor/Practitioner_____

Questions_____
_____
_____

Weight_____BloodPressure_____Pulse_____

Test Results_____

Answers_____
_____
_____
_____

Prenatal/Post-Partum Appointments

Date/Time_____Doctor/Practitioner_____

Questions_____
_____
_____

Weight_____BloodPressure_____Pulse_____

Test Results_____

Answers_____
_____
_____
_____

Prenatal/Post-Partum Appointments

Date/Time_____Doctor/Practitioner_____

Questions_____
_____
_____

Weight_____BloodPressure_____Pulse_____

Test Results_____

Answers_____
_____
_____
_____

Prenatal/Post-Partum Appointments

Date/Time_____Doctor/Practitioner_____

Questions_____
_____
_____

Weight_____BloodPressure_____Pulse_____

Test Results_____

Answers_____
_____
_____
_____

Prenatal/Post-Partum Appointments

Date/Time_____Doctor/Practitioner_____

Questions_____
_____
_____

Weight_____BloodPressure_____Pulse_____

Test Results_____

Answers_____
_____
_____
_____

Prenatal/Post-Partum Appointments

Date/Time_____Doctor/Practitioner_____

Questions_____
_____
_____

Weight_____BloodPressure_____Pulse_____

Test Results_____

Answers_____
_____
_____
_____

Prenatal/Post-Partum Appointments

Date/Time_____Doctor/Practitioner_____

Questions_____

_____

_____

Weight_____BloodPressure_____Pulse_____

Test Results_____

Answers_____

_____

_____

_____

Prenatal/Post-Partum Appointments

Date/Time_____Doctor/Practitioner_____

Questions_____

_____

_____

Weight_____BloodPressure_____Pulse_____

Test Results_____

Answers_____

_____

_____

_____

Prenatal/Post-Partum Appointments

Date/Time_____Doctor/Practitioner_____

Questions_____
_____
_____

Weight_____BloodPressure_____Pulse_____

Test Results_____

Answers_____
_____
_____
_____

Prenatal/Post-Partum Appointments

Date/Time_____Doctor/Practitioner_____

Questions_____
_____
_____

Weight_____BloodPressure_____Pulse_____

Test Results_____

Answers_____
_____
_____
_____

Prenatal/Post-Partum Appointments

Date/Time_____Doctor/Practitioner_____

Questions_____
_____
_____

Weight_____BloodPressure_____Pulse_____

Test Results_____

Answers_____
_____
_____
_____

Prenatal/Post-Partum Appointments

Date/Time_____Doctor/Practitioner_____

Questions_____
_____
_____

Weight_____BloodPressure_____Pulse_____

Test Results_____

Answers_____
_____
_____
_____

Prenatal/Post-Partum Appointments

Date/Time_____Doctor/Practitioner_____

Questions_____
_____
_____

Weight_____BloodPressure_____Pulse_____

Test Results_____

Answers_____
_____
_____
_____

Prenatal/Post-Partum Appointments

Date/Time_____Doctor/Practitioner_____

Questions_____
_____
_____

Weight_____BloodPressure_____Pulse_____

Test Results_____

Answers_____
_____
_____
_____

Glossary

Abstinence- the method of birth control that requires a choice of no sexual intercourse

Abortion-spontaneous death/killing through various procedures of a fetus or baby before live birth.

Adoption- placement of a child by birth parent to another who will be the future parent.

AIDS- Acquired Immunodeficency Syndrome is an automimmune disease that attacks the immune system. AIDS is usually transmitted through sexual, needles, or contaminated blood.

Analgesics- Numbing drugs often used during labor that manage pain while allowing mom to remain conscience.

Anemia- a condition in which your blood has decreased oxygen carrying ability as a result of low number of cells or a decrease in hemoglobin. Intake of iron in the diet can help prevent iron deficiency anemia.

Aneuploidy- a chromosomal abnormality where there are either extra or missing chromosomes. The most common cause of genetic disorders for example, Down syndrome.

Ante partum-a time from conception to labor.

Amniocentesis- a test usually carried out in the second trimester to look for fetal defects or fetal maturity. It is done by extracting amniotic fluid through mom's abdomen by a needle.

Amniotic fluid-The fluid that surrounds the fetus in the uterus.

Apagar score, scale or test- a test performed immediately after birth to assess the newborns' physical condition. Scored from a low of 0 to a high of a 10, test evaluates heart rate, respiratory effort, muscle tone, reflexes, and skin color. An ideal score is between 7-10

Bloody show- bloody discharge of mucus, which forms in the cervix and is shown right before or at the beginning or labor.

Braxton Hicks contractions- Irregular and hardening or painful contractions of the uterus, especially later in pregnancy. They are often mistaken for the start of labor and called "false labor".

Breech-the position of a baby that is upside down (bottom up feet down) in the uterus.

Caudal-a local anesthetic injected into the base of the spine to ease pain during labor and delivery.

Cervix-the neck shaped lower entrance to the uterus.

Cesarean section/surgery- Delivery of the baby through a cut in the abdominal and uterine walls. Usually done to protect the health of mother or child.

Colostrum- yellowish fluid rich in minerals that the baby needs. It is secreted by the breasts late in pregnancy and for the first couple of days after birth before mom's milk come in.

Contractions-the regular tightening of the muscles in the uterus as they work to open the cervix in labor and then push the baby down the birth canal.

Couvade syndrome- symptoms associated with pregnancy that is experienced by the father-to-be.

Down syndrome (Trisomy 21)- Genetic disorder caused by the presence of an extra chromosome and characterized by mental retardation, abnormal features of the face, and medical problems such as heart defects, Chances of your baby carrying this disorder increase with increasing age of mom. This can be tested for between 15 and 20 weeks pregnant with the Maternal Serum Analyte screen.

Dilation- the gradual opening of the cervix caused by contractions of the uterus during labor.

Doppler- device that allows your baby's heartbeat to be heard through a speaker

Doula-an assistant who provides various forms of non-medical support to women in childbirth process.

Effacement-the gradual opening of the cervical canal in the final month of pregnancy and into the first stage of labor. A measure of the progression of labor.

Embryo-the fertilized egg in the uterus from conception through the first eight weeks of development.

Engorgement-the overfilling of the breasts with milk

Epidural-a local anesthetic injected through a catheter into the epidural space in the lower spine to ease the pain during labor and delivery.

Episiotomy-a surgical cut made to enlarge the vagina to ease delivery.

Fetus- the unborn baby in the uterus from 8 weeks until birth.

Gestation-the time between conception and delivery

Gynecologist-a doctor specializing in female medicine.

Hypertension-high blood pressure that, in pregnancy, can be associated with many problems including reduced blood flow to the fetus.

Induced labor, or induction-the process of artificially starting labor

Jaundice- a yellowing of the skin of a newborn that occurs in about half of all births. It is caused by the immaturity of the newborns liver and is usually easily treated with bright light.

Kegals-exercise that strengthens the pelvic floor muscles.

Lactation- the production of milk by the breast.

Lamaze method-a birthing technique based on coached relaxation and breathing techniques that are synchronized to the expectant mothers contractions.

Leboyer method- a birthing method designed to created peaceful entry to the world for the baby: low light, immediate holding of the baby by mom, and a calm delivery room atmosphere. **Maternal Serum Analyte Screen**- Group of blood test, also known as quad screen, that check for substances linked with certain birth defects such as Down Syndrome, neural tube defects, Edward syndrome and other related birth defects, the test is done during the 15-21 weeks this test has many false positives.

Meconium-the dark green or black fecal matter present in the baby's bowel before birth and passed in the first few days after delivery.

Mucus plug-a stopper of cervical mucus that closes the opening of the cervix, It keeps the bacteria from entering into the cervix, providing a protective barrier for the baby. As the cervix opens the mucus plug may fall out. It may be noticed as a thick glob of stringy mucous, usually thicker then what is seen with normal vaginal secretions. Losing the mucus plug does not always mean labor will begin shortly. Call your doctor right away if you lose it before 36 weeks.

Neonatology- Branch of medicine that specializes in the care of ill or premature newborns

Neural tube Defect- birth defects that result from improper development of the brain, spinal cord, or their coverings. Tested between 15-21 weeks with a Maternal Serum Analyte screen blood test.

Oxytocin-a natural hormone that stimulates uterine contractions and the glands that produce breast milk.

Perinatal-the period from the 28 week of pregnancy to one week after birth

Placenta (after birth) - an organ of pregnancy attached to the wall of the uterus where oxygen, nutrients, and waste exchange takes place between the mother and the fetus. It usually delivers within 30 minutes of the baby birth.

Perineum- the area surrounding the vagina and between the vagina and rectum.

Pitocin-a synthetic form of the hormone oxytocin. Pitocin is used in artificially induced labor.

Postpartum-between birth and 6 weeks after delivery

Pre-eclampsia-a condition in pregnancy when blood pressure rises and protein in the urine increases. This increases the risk of seizures and other complications in the mother.

Prenatal- time between first being pregnant and before delivery

Show/bloody show- a bloody or pink vaginal discharge a few hours or days before the onset of labor and delivery.

Ultrasound-a diagnostic test used to assess baby's development, sex and health. A device that creates an image of the fetus from reflected high frequency sound waves.

Uterus- the hollow, muscular organ in the pelvic cavity where the fertilized egg implants and develops into the fetus.

Resources

Books

Eisenberg, Arlene, Heidi Murkoff, and Sandee Hathaway. What to Expect When You're Expecting. New York: Workman, 1992

Mueser, Anna, George Verrilli. While Waiting. New York: St Martin's Press, 1993

Rothman, Barbara Katz, ed. Encyclopedia of Childbearing. New York; Holt, 1993

Roundtree, Walter, Zand. Smart Medicine for a Healthier Child. New York: Penguin Group Second Edition, 2003

Neal Yard Remedies. Healing Foods. New York. First American Edition, 2013

Neal Yards Remedies. Natural Mother and Baby. New York. First American Edition

Web Sources

http://www.americanadoptions.com/adoption

Printed in the United States
By Bookmasters